ONLINE SECRETS FOR WOMEN BEGINNERS

12-MONTH FOR A SMOOTH TRANSITION FROM YOUR
JOB TO AN ONLINE BUSINESS, CRUSH LIMITING
BELIEFS, CREATE SECURITY, AND BUILD TRUE
FINANCIAL FREEDOM

KARINA G. SANCHEZ

Published by Virago Publishing
www.CorporateToFreelancer.com

Virago

PUBLISHING

DEDICATION

To every woman in the world, you deserve the best. May this book inspire you to conquer the highest mountains, cross the deepest rivers, and never give up on your dreams.

"Be Fearless In The Pursuit Of What Sets Your Soul On Fire."

– Jennifer Lee

A SPECIAL GIFT FOR YOU

DOWNLOAD YOUR GIFT NOW

2023 MONTHLY BUDGET
Get Organized

www.CorporateToFreelancer.com

QR CODE FOR YOUR SPECIAL GIFT

It's time to get your finances under control. When most of my clients do this simple money-tracking activity for 90 days, they can't believe how much money they find in places they never looked. One of the best skills you can learn is knowing exactly where your money is going. You can never be fully in control of your finances until you figure out the following:

1. How much money do you spend on your needs vs. your wants?
2. How much money are you saving monthly?
3. How much money are you wasting that you could be investing in yourself?

INTRODUCTION

> "Dream Big. Start Small. But Most of All, Start"
> ~ Simon Sinek

Ready to start your own online business with me as your coach? Tired of hustling 9-5 in your current job and getting nowhere? Want to do something more meaningful – something for you? Or simply sick of the daily grind and want to feel excited about your life again?

If you're screaming 'YES' right now, then you have just found the key to achieving your dreams. They start today. They start with this book!

Most of us have a secret desire burning inside us that drives us toward financial freedom so we can do the things we love and spend time with those we love. We want to elevate our financial status, and while some already have stable, well-paying job, we are looking for something more. We are looking to earn more money for more flexibility and freedom, and making the leap toward earning money online can be a struggle. It's overwhelming for most, so it's no wonder you feel insecure or haven't figured out how to shift from your day job into the online world.

There are so many barriers we face in life already. Many of us believe we're too old to start something new, creating an instant roadblock. We prevent ourselves from adjusting to the modern ways of making money, but the truth is, men and women all over the world are rising up, being brave, and boldly stepping into the world of online. There's no reason why you can't do it too, and 'no,' age is not a good excuse if that's the one you're using.

About two and a half years ago, I realized I was sick and tired of how exhausted I constantly felt. I was overworked and underpaid, but I was tired of having absolutely no work-life balance. I worked for the weekends, and I couldn't see a way out. The lack of flexibility got in the way of my family life. I had no energy, and I was always on the run. I was either running to drive my kids to the 1,000 places they had to go to (ok, exaggerating a little, but you know what I mean) or cooking, cleaning, and getting groceries, and that pretty much was my weekend. Come Monday morning, I would be running for the train to get to work and starting the crazy weekly commute once again. I was done. I knew there had to be more. While I wanted to make money online, I lacked direction, didn't know how to get where I wanted to be, and wanted to be free. I knew that by not keeping up with technology and new trends, I was at risk of becoming stale, and I feared I would miss my window of opportunity. I feared missing out on leveraging new opportunities to create *real wealth*. While I had the enthusiasm to join in with money-making opportunities online, I didn't have the know-how, and it was driving me insane – I was beginning to feel obsolete. Things had to change, so I had to become change-ready.

I know what it's like to be part of the rat race. To:

- Find it difficult to find time to do what you love.
- Feel like your dreams are much bigger than your pocket, or…
- Feel like you have no idea what you're doing and are just too afraid to try new things.

This was me until three years ago; I had a revelation. I was unhappy and needed to break free from never having enough. It was time to follow my true calling, teaching and educating people. Fast forward to today, I already have a number one best-selling book, which has helped many managers reach their dream positions. I'm now offering my online courses and running a successful online business.

As a keynote speaker and a corporate trainer, delivering sessions in English, Spanish, Portuguese, and Polish, I have facilitated hundreds of in-person and virtual workshops internationally over the last 15 years. I have lived worldwide and worked as a consultant in the pharmaceutical, retail, and financial industries – just to name a few. Just three years ago, I knew I had to leave my corporate job, and after my book became a bestseller, I took my knowledge and skills to the next level. After building my business to 6-figures in less than two years, I now show other amazing women of all ages and walks of life how to do the same.

If I can do it, YOU can too!

So, if you're ready to:

- Elevate your income by creating a rewarding avenue that provides a steady passive income.
- Learn the necessary skills to earn money online while working on your terms and starting your own online business.
- Get the flexibility you desire, feel more content, and finally achieve work-life balance and spend more time doing the things you love.
- Gain the confidence to make the right choices and feel more accomplished in everything you do so you can win your next client over and over.
- Leverage the modern ways to make money using technology, which allows you to connect with the world to capture global

opportunities. Don't let technology spook you; it's not that hard.

This book will show you how, and by the end, you will find the courage to take the first step toward the life you've been dreaming of. The life you want. The life you deserve. Together, we can make it happen. It will begin with an honest overview, so you crush the lies you've been telling yourself and overcome the excuses you keep placing in front of your way – because often, we are the biggest barrier to our success. You will then learn how to mentally prepare to run your business by first finding your 'why' and exploring what motivates you to pursue your dreams. You can then use that motivation to overcome the fear and make financial preparations to ensure you are secure when beginning your new venture. We'll then move on to developing your skills to help grow and develop your business, ensuring its future sustainability. In the final section, you'll settle on your niche and ensure you choose the right online business for you, from finding the right platform to increasing your customer base and embracing your flexibility by introducing passive income streams into your business.

Your knowledge and expertise give you the power to succeed as an entrepreneur. You must learn to leverage your skills correctly and position your business based on your strengths.

There's no time to waste, so if you're ready to begin crushing the ugly lies upfront and discovering how to overcome the excuses you're making that prevent you from starting your business, head over to chapter 1, and get unstuck right now. There is no time like the present. It's a gift. Don't waste it.

> *"The best way to predict the future is to create it."*
> *~ Peter Drucker*

SECTION I

Crushing All The False Beliefs Upfront

CRUSHING FALSE BELIEFS

*I*t's time to live your life to the fullest. You can do what you want to do or be who you want to be, and anything that stands in your way; you CAN overcome – there's always a way. Starting anything new is scary; believe me, I know because I did it, and I was scared. I would be lying to you if I told you otherwise. Because of fear, we sometimes can be a barrier to our own success. We make excuses that are often unfounded, but we make them anyway, preventing us from doing things that could bring us high levels of success.

How do we define an unfounded excuse?

In a nutshell, we tell ourselves lies that stop us in our tracks. If your dream is to start an online business, you owe it to yourself to at least do some research and look into it. We persuade ourselves that we can't pursue our dreams, and so we never do. It's time to stop because, in reality, 99% of the things you worry about will never happen, so stop wasting time because you don't have the luxury. I mean, what else do you have to do with the rest of your life? If you have another 40 to 60 years to live, wouldn't you want to do something fun with it? Business is fun. Yeah, it's challenging, but it's so rewarding, and the sense of accomplishment you will feel will make it all worth it in the end. I promise.

So, before you begin moving forward with your business, let's address the excuses. In this chapter, we're going to squash the six most common lies women tend to tell themselves.

Because what we want is possible. Even though we may not believe it at first...

Lie #1: I'm Too Old to Start. I Know Nothing About It

Be truthful with yourself - are you really too old to begin your business, or is this just an excuse based in fear?

There is a lot of noise regarding age and setting up your business. There are many positives that come with age, and yet, it's human nature to focus on the negatives. So many people believe that once they hit their 40-50s plus, they're much too old to change and adapt and therefore are much too old to start an online business.

It's not true because age gives you an advantage. It's called experience; believe me, you have much of it.

Many people start a business later in life. These days, the average age of an entrepreneur starting his/her business is 40 years old. Entrepreneurs around the age of 45 often set up the leading high-growth business start-ups. There are many people who begin successful and lucrative businesses post-retirement as well. Age doesn't put you at a disadvantage; it's the opposite.

At the age of 86, Sister Madonna Buder was still competing in Ironman and triathlons against people 50 years her junior. She didn't even begin running until she was 48 years old, which shows age doesn't have to be a barrier – so we must not let it. With age, we gain more experience and increase our expertise, so age is, in fact, an asset. It certainly helps us to become resilient and wise.

1. There are many benefits of starting a business when you're older. New entrepreneurs aged 40 plus also:
2. Have a bigger network, as you know more people and generally have more connections.
3. Are more familiar with accountability and can cope better with business responsibilities, challenges, and setbacks.
4. Have more life/work experience; over time, you have built on your expertise and matured in your line of work.

5. Generally, you have a more focused mindset and are ready to reach your goals and narrow down business objectives.
6. Have a better idea of your strengths and weaknesses, and have been able to practice using your strengths to get the job done.

Don't believe the age lie – you're simply limiting your success. Rather than recognizing everything you've done so far in life, you focus on the few things you haven't or don't know yet. This lie will lead you away from what could be an amazing business.

Lie #2: I don't have enough time. I already work full-time

Are you guilty of telling people how little time you have or how busy you constantly are?
Not having the time is a common excuse. I get it. When I started my online business, I had a full-time job and two teens to take care of on my own, so I know what busy means. Believe me. We say we work full-time, so we don't have time to go to the gym, so we let ourselves go. We don't have time to see our friends, so they forget us the next time they throw a party, and we ask why we weren't invited, or we don't have time to make a healthy meal, so we order out and gain weight. Well, being a business owner is all about utilizing your time and managing it effectively. If you master this skill, you'll soon see you do have time to do the things

that are important to you. That isn't to say that you don't have to commit time – of course, starting a business requires you to commit time, especially in the early stages. If it's important to you, you will find the time.

You can do some things to make more time to work on your business when you work full-time. You could:

- Wake up a little earlier and work on your business first thing in the morning.
- Set two-three goals or tasks each day in relation to your business, and get them done.
- Schedule in time throughout the week and/or weekend. Even if it's just a short time, that's okay. Always follow through with your plans. You will feel great.

As you begin to spend time on your business, it will start to feel real, and your excitement for your new project will increase. While you do have to put your time in, in the beginning, this will pay off later, so remind yourself of that. I recognize the importance of time management, so I dedicated a whole chapter to this topic in chapter 5. You'll soon be an expert in time management; therefore, this lie will be vanquished, as you'll no longer believe it.

Lie #3: You Need to Have Enough $$$ Saved Up Before You Can Quit Your Job

Do you believe you need thousands of dollars saved before you can quit your day job?

This is a claim made time and time again. People believe you need quite a bit of collateral to start a business. In fact, it's a common lie people tell themselves over and over again. People also believe you should save thousands of dollars to quit your job, but NO! it's simply not true. Maybe it is when you build a brick-and-mortar business, but an online business takes little or no investment.

While everyone's financial situation is different, you do not need to have massive amounts of money saved to start an online business or quit your job, regardless of what others may think. You only need to replace the bare minimum amount of money you need to cover your bills and food.

Some people do prefer to have a month or two of money saved in advance when they first quit their job and go into business, as it provides them with a little bit of security, just to be on the safe side. This is not necessary if you set your business up the right way, so you have a consistent income, and this way, you may not need to wait or dip into your savings.

In life, we have to take risks and go all in. If you spend your time and effort on your business full-time when you've previously only committed a few hours per week, you will see the difference reflected in your income. The details are often in the planning, so as long as you plan, you should be able to quit your job with minimal money; in fact, many people begin with very little or no money.

Lie #4: There Is Too Much Competition

Does the competition put you off when it comes to starting your business?

If it does, it shouldn't. You can use the competition much to your advantage when it comes to starting a business, yet this is another lie many people believe, and they use it as an excuse not to start up. Competition is good for any business, and it's up to you to ensure you run a unique business that sells unique products or services.

First, it's important that you see the value of competition. If we have competitors in the market, then we know how to measure our own business, and this also gives you insight into what products or services are currently in demand. Knowing your competitors helps your business in many ways. You can see what other businesses are doing, and while your business should never be the same exactly, it still provides you with a basic model to work from, and then you can figure out your unique selling point to offer your clients something more. Something extra. This ensures your business stands out from others. Remember, at the end of the day, your business will be successful if you provide value to your customers. Whether it's a product or a service, if they see the value, they will buy it. Focus on what it is that you will do for THEM. How will you make their life easier? What can they learn from you that ultimately will provide them with freedom, money, knowledge, etc.?

> *"When you help others be successful, you will become rich beyond your wild imagination."*
> ~ Oprah Winfrey

Telling ourselves, there is too much competition is a feeble excuse not to start a business. It just means you will have to work harder at providing *real value*. If your product or service is so good that everyone wants it, you will never have to worry about your competition. It's time to stop believing the lie and embrace the positives your competitors bring. It allows you to differentiate products and services, make good pricing decisions for your business, and penetrate an already productive market. There's no such thing as too much competition because there is so much variety in business and so much buying power. If you're an online business, you can appeal to your customers worldwide, and there are plenty of customers for everyone. When I published my first book in such a saturated niche, everyone told me not to do it, but this was my dream, and I was not about to let others crush it, so I worked hard. I wrote a book that was better than what was available on Amazon for my audience, and low and beholds; I did really well. Women loved the book, and it became the #1 Bestseller in Leadership. I would not have had a #1 best-selling book today if I had believed the' too much competition' lie. On Amazon alone, you have over 156 million customers. You are richer beyond your wildest dreams if you make even 0.000001 % of 156 million.

There are approximately 8 billion people worldwide – so you do the math!

Lie #5: No One Will Hire Me. I Don't Have Any Skills I Can Market

Believing that you don't have skills you can market is the biggest lie of all. This is an issue with one's self-belief and is not a legitimate excuse. If your boss has hired you, there's no reason why you can't be hired as an entrepreneur, only this time, it's on your terms. Think about the skills you were able to use to contribute to your job. What are you really good at? What comes naturally to you, and others always ask you to help them? Don't discount anything here.

So many people believe that nobody will hire them, and this is often because they lack confidence and don't believe in their own skill set and expertise or that these skills can help others. If you have a career, then you have skills. You have knowledge and skills if you have a hobby or something you know a lot about. All of these can help you when starting your business. If you complete the little exercise below and debunk this lie, you'll soon realize how much you have to offer.

Take a moment to brain-dump the information below – this can only be for your own eyes if you wish.

List everything, even the stuff you think no one would care about or need. If you want to go one step further, ask 2-3 people that know you really well to list the qualities you have that they rely on you for. You should list the following:

- All your qualities - friends
- All your qualifications - you
- All your work experience - you
- All the jobs you've had - you
- All the hobbies/passions you have - you
- Other things you know well or can do - you

For some people, this may take a while as we accumulate a lot of knowledge, skills, and experience over time. For example, if you're a parent, you know about pregnancy, birth, raising kids, discipline, time management, organization, etc. These women know more about this topic than a person looking to get pregnant or a parent for the first time. You can then start to narrow down your list by identifying the things you are most passionate about.

This is an excellent way to stop this lie in its tracks because most people are shocked by the size of the list they create from this exercise. I guarantee you know more than you think you do!

Lie #6: You Can't Because It's Not Possible

Most people don't believe it's possible to start on

their own for many reasons we've already discussed; for example, people feel they don't have the time or money. As we know, we can continue to make excuses, but if you haven't worked it out already, we make these excuses and believe these lies due to motivation and self-belief issues.

The idea that it's not possible for us to start a business often springs to mind first because it's not something we've truly considered. This is not because it's impossible, but rather than figuring out 'how' we can start our own business and considering the idea, we would rather take the easy path and rebuke it, accepting instant defeat.

The truth is that anyone can become an entrepreneur, but the belief must come from within, and many people do not believe it to be true, so they close themselves off from the idea and refuse to look into it further.

Unsuccessful people often think things are impossible because they don't know where to begin, fear failure, or aren't willing to put the work in. Starting a business is far from easy. It requires endurance, resilience, and commitment, but it requires willingness because everything else you can learn. It takes grit, not a genius, to be successful. If you can stick it out and push through the fear, you can have a very successful online business. Some feel they lack the skills, leadership, and knowledge needed to run a successful business, and while running a business is a bit of a learning curve at times, it's important to know that if you want it, it is certainly possible. You must want it, though, and you must be willing to commit. So, are you committed?

If your answer is YES, then nothing is impossible, and you can achieve your dreams!

Time for Motivation!

Motivation is extremely important when you're a business owner because you generally only have yourself to motivate. Let's finish this first chapter with three extremely powerful affirmations. Repeat them three to four times throughout your day – morning, noon, evening, and before going to sleep. Drift off being grateful.

1. I am grateful for the wealth and opportunities that come my way
2. I'm ready for another productive day, and I'm motivated to succeed
3. I am committed to setting up my business and making it a success

And the last one I like to start and end my day with goes something like this:

"Show Me How Good It Can Get"

Send that thought into the Universe daily, and it will show you exactly how good it can get today and every day. Try it. It's life-changing.

Now that you've squashed the lies you believed when running your own business, you can start making the necessary mental preparations. In the next chapter, we'll discuss your 'why' and figure out what motivates you to run your business. Your 'why' will be there when you feel down, lack energy or motivation, or when things get tough. Remember, you can do hard things. It's all just a learning curve. Once you know it, you can 'rinse and repeat.' All is well. All is doable.

SECTION II

Mentally Preparing For Liftoff

2

FIND YOUR "WHY"

> "Never doubt that you are valuable and powerful and deserving of every chance and opportunity in the world to pursue and achieve your dreams."
> ~ Hillary Clinton

Something about running a business online just makes sense to me... I felt like that for quite some time before I acted, and when I look back now, I wonder why it took me so long.

The online world has provided us with endless possibilities for making money, but there's so much more to it than that. While the opportunities have been there for several years, they grow and get bigger as time goes on because more people than ever before work from home and have discovered that they no longer want to suffer through commutes and waste precious time.

Of course, this was ultimately kick-started in 2020 by 2 years of lockdowns and travel restrictions caused by an unexpected pandemic. The demand for online services has exploded, and since then, it's maintained a steady pace as it's proved to be a great solution for so many people due to the opportunities it offers.

It's time for you to take advantage of these opportunities.

When the COVID-19 pandemic hit, it definitely impacted the whole world. It was a difficult time that pushed many people into working digitally since so many lost their jobs, but it's in our nature to adapt and change, so over time, more and more people began to embrace it.

People who we never thought would embrace the online world mastered it, including corporate professionals, our parents, grandparents, and children. If you craved human contact other than with the people you lived with, online was the only way. While this was challenging and wasn't the same as seeing people in person, we adapted, creating a digital revolution never seen before.

Entrepreneurs had to quickly rethink how they conduct their daily business and lean into new ways of running it. While some people struggled and yearned to return to a sense of normality, many adapted and saw the benefits of such working conditions. Many people started to prefer this as it gave them options and created new possibilities. Personally, for me, the world of online opened so many doors. Not only can I work from the location of my choice, but I can also work with people all over the world, and when your client reach increases to such a level, the money follows.

So many people lost the jobs they'd once deemed as 'safe,' and whole economies were affected by the pandemic, which meant that entrepreneurship was the only option for some. While being an entrepreneur is always a risk, the level of online clients within my grasp lessened that risk for me, and when it came to having a job, nobody was safe. Let's be honest; the pandemic ended the false belief that having a full-time job was safe. When I lost my job 2.5 years ago, I decided I would never rely on an employer again, and that decision kicked off my consulting career after close to 15 years in the corporate world. Now, I no longer rely on a job; I simply rely on the world of online, my expertise and resilience, and the millions (if not billions) of potential clients that need my service or product.

Digital technology has played a critical role in the creation of new businesses. It has been able to help revive and uplift new businesses while innovating new, creative ideas. While COVID-19 disrupted our lives, the online world gave us an edge, so we could still work, allowing us to fulfill our goals.

Before the pandemic, many businesses had started to make a shift to online, but there was always the fear that not all business clients would make the switch. The truth is that now more people have embraced it, and many businesses can run in a more sustainable way. This makes economic recovery so much more likely.

The aim of this chapter is to help you discover how you can make the switch to working as a freelancer and what benefits this brings. To work this out, you must figure out what motivates and drives you...

So, here's my question: What's your 'why'? Really.

Top Reasons to Become an Online Entrepreneur

Online businesses are shaping the world because of the many benefits of working for yourself. I help professional women transition from their corporate job to online business owners. While this is something I have always wanted to do, I was given a push when I lost my corporate job following the pandemic. I felt scared. I have bills to pay, a single mom, and other financial responsibilities, so making the leap wasn't easy. Regardless, I did it! I have had enough of being told how far I can climb up that ladder that never seemed to go anywhere. I knew I had a strong work ethic and would be able to bring that to my own business, and I did. The rest is history. This also gave me an opportunity to be completely financially independent. As a single mom, I have kids to take care of, and even though their dad is very involved and supportive, I have this need to be in complete control of my life. I want to be able to support myself financially. I want to call the shots, and I won't be able to do that until my business runs on automatic.

So, I had to prepare because I had to figure out how

to make my business work. I knew I would never allow myself to be in this situation again, and to be honest, I was tired of other people telling me what I could earn and how useful I was. I am an expert in my field, and I was swimming in life/work experience and skills I used for many years daily. It was my time. I'd wanted to pursue a career working for myself for so long, I could taste it, but I was too afraid to just go for it. Losing my job gave me the push. I wanted it, but the pressure was on – I had to make it work.

If other women could do it, *why not me?*

Businesses like Amazon and platforms like Zoom have revolutionized the world of online and have increased their market dominance as a result. Such technological changes forged the way and allowed us to change the rules. We could still have meetings, be educated, or conduct our business without being in the same room with other people. *I mean, imagine what life would've been like without those things during the pandemic.*

Even now, as the situation has improved, many people and businesses have continued to work with digital technologies because it makes things so much easier. The internet has reshaped the way we market and advertise our business. The online world has provided us with powerful platforms that allow us to communicate and get our message across.

Social media shows its dominance by allowing us to communicate with our potential and current clients daily, and it's easier for others to find us. Basically, when a person shares your online material, it is similar to a customer referring you to others.

Everything from how we shop to how we process data or manage our business processes has changed due to the power of being online. Even businesses that do not solely conduct their business online still have an online presence because it's necessary if they want to grow. We're in a new era of online business, and you can be part of this.

There are many reasons why you should become an online entrepreneur:

1. You are your own boss – ultimately, you make the rules. You can choose what work you take on or turn down. You can alter your day to fit around you, your life, and your family. You literally make the rules, so you have freedom and flexibility!

2. Low start-up costs – most online businesses require little or no capital. There are so many fees and expenses when you start a brick-and-mortar business, but with an online business, you have very little overhead. Sometimes, a laptop and an internet connection are all required.

3. The online world is filled with potential clients – when you're an online business, you're still catering to your online client, but you're marketing to the world without

traveling. Imagine how this increases your customer reach!

4. There is no limit to your earnings – the amount you earn is basically up to you; there is no limit to your income. You get to pick how much you WANT to earn, and you work towards it. You can choose what to charge and how to market your products or services. You're in complete control.

5. You'll have more free time – while you'll have to put a lot of time into your business, especially at the start, ultimately, you can begin to work towards reducing the time you work, which will free up more time for you. Even when you're putting in extra hours in the beginning, you still have the flexibility to work the hours you choose. Nobody tells you when to work and when not to – you're the boss!

6. You get to do the job you love – ultimately, if you're an onlinepreneur, it's likely that you're doing the job you love. You'll utilize the skills you have and enjoy your work. You might not love everything about entrepreneurship, but once you build your business, you can hire others to do the jobs you're less passionate about (see the next reason).

7. You create jobs for others – as well as working in a rewarding job that you love, you can create jobs for others. Let's say you don't

enjoy the parts of the business that involve finance, social media, or sales... You could hire someone for a few hours each week to do that. They are called VA's virtual assistants. That way, you're creating work for other people within your business, which has a positive economic impact.

8. There are incredible opportunities to scale and grow – while I can't guarantee you'll be an automatic success online, there are still many growth opportunities online. If you market your business well and have good brand recognition, you could start small and grow over time. Some businesses snowball into something larger than they ever expected.

9. Freedom is one of the most common reasons for starting a business. We all want to be able to pick and choose – who we do business with, how we do business, where we do it, and when. Working for yourself allows this, but remember, you only get what you put in from your business. With that in mind, make sure you don't confuse freedom with slacking off. You still need to do the work.

If some or all of these reasons sound good or resonate with you, it's important you take a step towards figuring out how to start your own business and do the things you love, the things you are destined to do. Working online can be so fun and fulfilling, but before you can begin, you need to understand and commit to your 'why' fully...

There's a reason attached to every decision you make, so before you move on to the next section, just take a moment to consider the question below:

What's your reason for shifting from corporate to an online business?

Finding Your Why

More and more people are choosing the freelancing life over their full-time corporate jobs. In fact, since COVID-19 hit, recent times have been referred to as *The Great Resignation* due to the number of people leaving their 9-5 jobs and going solo. We've discussed some of the top reasons above. Still, the truth is, people want to know that it's possible to earn more money, they want more freedom, and they want to be in the driving seat so that they can take advantage of every opportunity that crosses their path, but most of all, they want to recognize their true value.

Sound familiar?

When you work in the corporate world, people constantly tell you what to do, how to perform, and how much they will pay you. I remember feeling undervalued; when other people undervalue you, you lack your sense of worth. In such jobs, you are constantly working to please others, and you don't have the freedom and flexibility to express your full potential. Decisions are made on your behalf, yet once you get too close to the top of the corporate ladder, that's it. You're stuck. There are no more opportunities. You stagnate, and eventually, you get bored and leave anyway. You repeat this cycle until you are old and have no more energy to live your life to the fullest. It's soul-wrenching.

But it doesn't have to be that way because you don't have to let it. You have the power to change it!

Do you know why you want to switch to having an online business? Do any of the reasons discussed in this chapter so far resonate with you?

Although money isn't everything, it does make our lives easier, but it's important to get the right formula. If you get enjoyment and fulfillment from your work, it provides you with flexibility and freedom, then the money you make (and keep on making) is a bonus. But of course, that bonus brings its own benefits too. I want you to really think about your reasons because it's important you become the entrepreneur you want and need to be – one that never stops helping others succeed. Money is an important reason, but yet, people shy away from it, like the idea of wanting more money is embarrassing or something dirty we should be ashamed of. Don't be. If it's the money you want, fantastic! I'm happy for you! I want it too! *Let's scream it out loud! I want more money!* Now that we know what we want, what value can we provide to our customers to help them get what they want?

So, what's the difference between a successful freelancer and one that no one hires?

Successful freelancers recognize their strengths and can utilize them in their work. They are ready and able to produce steady income streams and are motivated by their creative side. They are focused on their goals and are ready to make the shift. But it's not always easy to get to this stage. It's something you have to recognize first.

Transitioning from a full-time career to an online business boss is a challenge, especially if you want to set yourself up for life by being super-successful. As an entrepreneur, it's your responsibility to grow your business and ensure it's lucrative, but you're only going to be able to do this if you're clear about your 'why.'

Freelancing does not come without risk and can be unpredictable at times. When you first branch out, it can be scary as your income may not be stable, and getting it to a stable level can be tricky. The key to success is preparing mentally, financially, and physically. Having a long-term vision will help you develop grit, taking you further than you ever thought possible.

As a freelancer, you must be persistent and patient, and you must put the work in, but as mentioned before, you must stay motivated and recognize your own value. While most entrepreneurs know what their business does and how they need to conduct their business, they don't know the 'why' behind it all. Your 'why' is your purpose. It is the very essence behind your business – the very reason it exists.

To figure out your 'why,' it's a good idea to consider a series of questions. Ask yourself:

- When it comes to freelancing, what's important to me (this could be your career, money, spending time with your family, your freedom, or flexibility)?
- What inspired my business idea?
- What am I passionate about? Does it resonate with my business?
- What are my core beliefs and values – both personally and professionally?
- Why does my business exist (what purpose does it serve)?
- Why do I want to be an entrepreneur? What drives me?
- What sets my business apart from others?
- What skills can I incorporate into my business and help others succeed?

I wanted more freedom, flexibility, and more time with my family, but I also wanted to earn more money. As a single mom, I struggled to make ends meet, so I wanted to build a business that would allow me to have the freedom to buy what I wanted when I wanted for my kids. I'd hit the income ceiling in my corporate career, and the thought of not being able to increase my earnings to the level I wanted wasn't good enough for me. This helped me forge my business story, which is integral to what I do. People often buy from the people they can relate to, and that's what happened to me. I became a beacon of hope for other women like me, and I wouldn't have it any other way.

Your 'why' makes you unique, which can make all the difference between a client buying from you or never looking you up again.

What's your 'why'? Have you figured it out yet?

In 2022, being an online business entrepreneur is becoming more and more desirable as people want to improve their skill sets, they want to take advantage of being able to travel and work from a destination of their choice, and the fact that they no longer have to follow the corporate dress code is just a bonus. Freelancers set their own terms in business.

Once you know your 'why,' you're still afraid of going solo. If you have a stable corporate job, becoming an entrepreneur is not something you'll want to jump into, feet first… Preparation is a must.

But before we move on to that, how do you overcome your fears?

Let's find out in chapter 3!

3

GET PAST THE FEAR AND GO AFTER WHAT YOU LOVE

"Face your fears as if your life depends on it, because living in fear keeps you from living."
~ *Jeanette Coron*

ear stops us in our tracks. It's debilitating. It prevents us from achieving our goals and going for what we want in life. If you want to go after what you desire most, you must learn to overcome your fears!

In this chapter, we'll learn how to get past our fears so we can confidently chase our passions. You'll explore how fear affects you, the science behind the fear, as well as consider how you can tackle your fear head-on. We'll also talk through strategies you can use to overcome the barriers of fear that are standing in your way and blocking your future.

So, how exactly does fear work?

The Science of Fear

Fear is complex yet powerful. It's part of our human nature to constantly assess the dangers or threats we perceive as we carry on with everyday life. While it's okay if you face real threats, if you're being paralyzed with fear to the point that you can't move forward, you'll need to look at that closely and figure out what's more important. The fear or your dream life? You will need to decide and just take the first step forward.

Fear is how your body reacts to danger and prepares you for it, although it's an emotion that's not always easy to control. When we start to sense danger, hormones are released into the body. This kick-starts certain body functions; for example, our heart races and pumps blood to muscles, which means we can run faster if needed. It also shuts down or slows down some of our other systems temporarily that it views as non-essential, as it goes into survival mode. That fear is then stored in our memory, and as the body also increases the flow of hormones to the brain, we focus solely on the danger.

Fear sometimes takes hold because we have doubts or feel anxious about something. You can relate this to how you feel about leaving behind stable employment for entrepreneurship. Fear may be preventing you from taking the leap, as for many years, it held me back until I learned to lean into it rather than try to run away from it. I couldn't find the strength to make the leap because there were too many 'unknowns' stopping me. I knew I couldn't let it stop me this time because my 'why' was much stronger than my fear. So instead of running, I breathed.

Fear is not just emotional; it's biochemical. When your survival mode kicks in, you will experience an actual physical reaction, such as rapid heart rate, sweating, and increased adrenaline. This means you are extremely alert. This is referred to as your 'fight or flight' instinct because, at this stage, you are ready to either flee or prepare for combat. It becomes out of control when we don't deal with our fear head-on. This soon turns into chronic fear, which has further serious consequences.

Chronic fear impacts our physical health, memory, brain processing, reactions, and mental health, which means we are unable to function to the best of our ability, and sometimes, we are unable to be rational. Let's quickly explore how this happens:

- Fear negatively impacts our physical health because it weakens our immune system. It also causes issues with the heart and stomach, decreases fertility, and it makes us feel old. Who wants to feel old? Not me!
- It impairs our memory and impacts parts of the brain that allow us to regulate our fear. This means it's difficult to manage your fear, leaving you anxious.

- It also interrupts how your brain processes and regulates emotions. It prevents you from effectively reading non-verbal cues and misunderstanding any other information communicated to us. This means we can act in an irrational way as it can be difficult for us to make decisions; it will cause us to react impulsively and fire up intense emotions.
- Our mental health is also at risk when it comes to long-term fear, as this often leads to anxiety or depression, fatigue, and it can even result in PTSD.

Becoming an entrepreneur doesn't come without risk. Anxiety and fear are something we feel as a result. Some things are riskier than others, so the level of risk can impact how we feel about it – *what do we have to lose?* Some people have more to lose than others, but these feelings of anxiety and fear are generally normal. However, if you feel overly scared or anxious, it is possible that such feelings can be caused due to a traumatic event from your past rooted in your memory. As we go through life, there are certain things that trigger anxiety and fear that stem from our past. There are several reasons why this may happen, and there is also an argument that suggests that it can be a part of our genetic makeup, generational fear if you will.

We develop chronic fear because we don't deal with our anxiety and the feelings of fear and allow them to escalate to the point where they become paralyzing.

This can cause mental health conditions to arise or spiral. If you're persistently worrying about situations that occur every day but don't approach a problem logically, it can become more intense and excessive.

One of the key fears people suffer from when it comes to business is the fear of success. When I dug deep, I wasn't wholly comfortable with this. The idea of success can be scary, so I put blocks up in an attempt to protect myself.

This sounds crazy, right?

It's easy for you to be your own barrier regarding your business. Women, in particular, are often hard on themselves. They stand in their own way and see problems as failures rather than spending time thinking of how to overcome or find a way around them. This often prevents us from heading in the direction we need to go, but this need not be permanent. We may just need to take a slightly longer path to get to our destination, kind of like when you're at the airport and your flight is canceled, so you have to take a slight detour. You're not done; your route simply changes.

Let's move on to the next section and focus on how to face our fears in more detail.

Facing Your Fears

When you fear success, it holds you back in business and in life. It's a self-sabotage of sorts, and while it's likely you don't do this on purpose, there is usually some underlying issue. You may not believe you're incapable of success but may fear the idea of change itself. Fearing success happens in many forms, for example:

- Some people feel that public success may mean emotional or social isolation.
- Some people are uncomfortable being in the spotlight and fear the extra attention.
- Some are worried that they'll be seen as someone who is bragging or showing off.
- Some people feel celebrating success is self-promotion and aren't comfortable doing that.
- Success is not always what you think it is.
- You may feel your achievements will push you away from your peers.
- When you're high up on the pedestal (that you didn't want to be on in the first place), you fear you might get knocked from it at some point, and that's frightening.
- You fear what will happen if you fail.

If you fear success, you probably have low goals, are self-destructive, quit even though success is within your grasp, you procrastinate, which means opportunities pass you by, or you may even constantly feel the need to strive for perfection. If things aren't perfect, you see this as a failure. and stop. This is a vicious trap to fall into because such behaviors prevent you from reaching your full potential.

As business owners, we're encouraged to show up as the best versions of ourselves, but with this comes a lot of pressure, feelings of anxiousness, and guilt. It's important you don't let these feelings overwhelm you.

In business, many people suffer from imposter syndrome, which puts doubt in their minds. This means you must work on yourself but take the first step once you identify your fears. You can then problem-solve each one and work out strategies to overcome everything and anything that stands in your way.

5 Tips For Overcoming Your Fear Of Success:

1. Explore the origins of your fear by asking 'why' you feel this way. Try to examine your past experiences – *when was the first time you remember experiencing this fear?*
2. Make a list indicating how you've been sabotaging your success. Writing it down gives you focus, so you can begin to figure out how to approach this problem.
3. Try visualizing your ideal life and what your successes would provide. Allow these images to fill you with happiness. Imagine achieving your goal and think about what would you do with your success.
4. Manage your anxiety and stress by taking care of yourself first. Take time to relax, eat a

balanced diet, exercise daily, even if it's a 10-minute stretch, and spend time with friends and family. You may go further by reading, meditating, and writing in a journal or give back to the community by volunteering. Believe me; there is always someone worse off than you. It puts things in perspective.

5. Get help from a professional if you need it – you don't have to do it alone. I have a psychologist I go to just to vent because I hate venting to my friends. They don't know what to do, and it's not fair. Sometimes, if we feel overwhelmed and truly fear success, working on our own can be a struggle. You could see a therapist as I do, or you could work with a success coach, which I have as well. Every entrepreneur has a coach because it's important to learn from people who have already accomplished a certain level of success that you want to get yourself. Why not learn from those who have already done it? Other professionals will help you cope and handle your success better while helping you get to the root cause. A therapist will help get to the root of the matter. This will allow you to manage the fear itself better.

Your fears tend to mask themselves, so they are not so obvious, so don't beat yourself up if you don't realize the root cause instantly. If you keep working on facing your fears, you will overcome that nagging fear of success and learn to recognize it and deal with it. It takes time and practice, but it becomes second nature once you overcome your fears and face them head-on.

Unlocking the Mental Doors

Moving past your fears is difficult, but you must conquer them. We create mental blocks because our fear keeps us safe, so if you really want to begin releasing your fears, you must first identify what they are so you can assess why they're there in the first place. Get quiet. Meditate on it for a while. Write it down, then break it down. Be as specific as possible!

We take such a negative outlook when it comes to fear, but it's important you remember that fear can sometimes be a good thing, and you can use it to increase your alertness, fire up your motivation, and give you an edge. You can also use your fear to guide your intuition because without it, *how would you sense danger or assess risks?*

Sometimes, fear works in our favor, and it's important you recognize when it does.

What does success look like if you want to move past your fears, set achievable goals, imagine your ideal outcome, and then schedule time daily to work towards it? Commit to the goals and put clear steps in place that will take you toward that goal. Ensure you are clear and realistic when you set these – the more specific, the better.

Fear can make us avoid certain tasks, so stay in tune with how you feel and recognize the excuses you make that prevent your progress. Ask yourself why you're making excuses because you won't move forward if you're not addressing the whole issue.

If you truly want success, it's time to adopt a growth mindset. This mindset allows you to grow, and it's one of the most powerful things you can do if you want to overcome your anxiety and fear. You don't need to achieve your goals every time, but it's important to get out of your comfort zone at times and then continue, regardless of any mistakes or barriers you face. Stagnating when you feel fear is easy, so be sure you know how to keep going. Most people give up when they are only 2 centimeters (1 inch) away from success. Think about it. That's why most people never become successful.

Success becomes more difficult if you're hanging out with the wrong people. People who lack the motivation to strive for success will suck your energy. Remember, you deserve better, so you must stand up for yourself and start making new friends.

Surround yourself with successful people and others who are committed to getting what they want in life but will also push you to achieve your own dreams. Get these people to hold you *accountable,* and don't forget to raise your standards – it's time to really push yourself to ensure you reach your goals.

Failure is a concept you either believe in or you don't. You will make the choice. Either way, you're right. Think about that. Failure is NOT an option – so from now on, it's no longer a word in your vocabulary. Accept that you won't always achieve what you want to achieve when you want to achieve it, and you may need to alter your path. Forgive yourself! This doesn't mean you've failed; you have to problem-solve and overcome the barriers blocking the path – you're simply changing your course a little.

If you start small and have faith, you'll get to where you want to be. This is a journey, not a destination, and it's certainly not a 'get rich quick scheme.' Simply learn to accept when ideas develop or don't and move on regardless of the outcome. One of the biggest worries when becoming a freelancer is money. That's why, in the next chapter, we'll talk about how you can prepare yourself financially so that when you quit your job, you don't have to worry about how you'll pay your bills.

Now, let's talk about money!

4

PREPARING FINANCIALLY
BEFORE YOU QUIT YOUR JOB

One of your biggest concerns when setting up a business is your financial stability. It can be difficult to decide when to quit your job and jump all in, especially if you have responsibilities. I pondered this decision for some time, but when I lost my job, I had a choice…

Do I go back into the corporate world, or do I take the chance and put everything into my business? That was the question.

I didn't want to get stuck in another job I didn't really want. I knew the business had to work, but that didn't mean I didn't prepare financially – I have my kids to take care of and financial responsibilities I could not ignore. It's a big leap and can certainly be scary!

In this chapter, I'll talk you through the signs that suggest it's time to quit your job. I'll also explore what you need to do before you put in that resignation and provide tips on how to secure your finances first while providing you with budgeting tips to ensure you manage your finances effectively.

Let's begin your journey to financial security...

When is the Best Time to Quit My Job?

When we decide we want to start our own business, we feel excited, and we are invested in the idea. We want it to happen NOW!

But...

While the motivation and excitement we feel are important, it's equally as important that we don't jump in without thinking. If you want your new business to succeed, you must ensure its longevity.

It's easy to make rash decisions in the heat of the moment, but when it comes to your career, you need to act cautiously. Now, you're obviously starting a business for a reason, and you're clear about your why, but when we make big business decisions, we need to do this logically and strategically.

Is it ever the right time to quit your job?

This is an interesting question because arguments are always for and against it, and you need to look at both sides. The warning signs that tell you it's time to look for something better include:

- You've achieved what you wanted to – if like me, you hit the glass ceiling and feel there are no further prospects or growth opportunities for you, it may be time to consider what you want to do next. If you got to where you want to be and there's nothing more, that's generally a dead giveaway; it's time to go.
- You're actively looking for ways to avoid your job – firstly, don't confuse this with being work-shy. This means you're good at your job but crave something else. You've started procrastinating and lack interest and passion in your work. You'd rather do anything else, other than your job because the enjoyment is gone… It's time to review your career and consider what you are passionate about. *What's your ideal job? What do you want to do instead? Do you have a nagging passion that won't let you sleep at night?*
- There are no opportunities to grow – we link to this a little when we talk about achieving the things we've wanted to achieve, but if there's nothing left… There are no other areas of the business to learn about, no skills to develop, and no opportunity for promotion or growth; maybe it's time to move on.
- If you're starting to develop bad habits due to your job – some businesses aren't the best to work for and create a culture of toxicity that

doesn't serve the business or its employees. Suppose that's the case, and you're finding yourself being dragged into unethical, inappropriate, or untruthful settings. In that case, it may be time to move on, especially if those things diverge you from your values and purpose. You should never allow a professional environment to have a negative impact on you.

- Your employer isn't interested in your career goals – if your employer won't support your goals and shuts you down, it's likely that you will have no future with that company.

- The workplace is harming your physical or emotional health (or both). If the workplace puts performance before its employees and piling on the pressure to achieve unrealistic and unfair goals, it could be time to look for another job. If you're personally insulted, stressed, and massively overworked, this is not a positive working environment and will make you less productive in the future, possibly causing health issues.

- The company is struggling – if the company or industry you're working in is struggling, it may be best to weigh your options and find a more stable working environment. Sometimes, we can't control what goes on around us or in the market, so ensure you're in a stable position or move on.

This is just a little taste of the warning signs you may experience that suggest it's time to move on from your current job. You could look for something else, or maybe, it's time to start your own business. That business you've been dreaming of! There may be other signs too, but only you can read them and make the decision... Go with your gut.

Is it time to acknowledge these signs and turn them into an opportunity, or do you simply ignore them?

I say, go for it. You deserve more. But while we've discussed the best time to quit your job, *when shouldn't we do it?*

When is the Worst Time to Quit My Job?

Sometimes you shouldn't just quit your job, as it may not be the right move right now. While it may be tempting and quite empowering to head into your workplace one day and hand in your notice, it isn't that simple. Think twice about quitting your job if:

- You don't have any savings at all – it's too risky to quit if you don't have any means to pay your bills or keep up with your financial responsibilities. You'd simply be left both penniless and jobless.
- You don't have a plan – while you don't need a job lined up exactly, you do need to plan

what's next for you. *Where will you go from here? What will you do?*

- There are some barriers to overcome – leaving your job for the right reasons is important. If you're having a difficult period at work, consider if this is how it always is or if it's just simply a moment that will soon pass. Sometimes, if we wait things out, we're glad we persevered in our role, as small or growing businesses can experience a lot of change all at once, but soon after, things calm down. Just make sure it's what you really want and not just a bump in the road because when you decide to quit, there'll be no regrets.

- You're chasing money – while money is nice, it's the wrong focus. A high-paying job is physically and mentally stressful. More money will undoubtedly bring more working hours or a tougher work environment, which you might not like. You will have to make sure it's what you really want. Focus on helping others instead.

- You're not making sound decisions – sometimes, something happens, and it's hard to think clearly. It causes us to act on our emotions, which means we're not thinking straight, and we act on a whim. Don't just quit because you're angry or upset. Sleep on it first. Think it through before you make any decisions you might regret.

- You haven't spoken to your boss to see if you can get what you want – a lot of companies value their employees, and therefore, they try their best to accommodate requests and offer growth opportunities. You don't know until you ask. So, ask. Don't quit until you've made your requests clear and you have allowed them to react.

Only you can make the decision regarding your resignation, so ensure you think this through first. While we're on this subject, let's talk about what you need to do when you resign.

What Should You Do Before Putting in Your Resignation?

Putting in your resignation is pretty stressful. So many people are quitting as part of 'The Great Resignation,' but there are some things you need to do first – to make sure you've considered everything.

1. Make sure you've checked out your options with your current employer – if you enjoy your work, try to negotiate new terms. Consider promotions, arrangements for flexibility, such as working from home, or future opportunities or training. Some people

request to reduce their work hours to start their own business part-time. Check with your human resources department on this one first.

2. Imagine your ideal job. Now, put together your ideal job description – start with your overall career goal, and write down what you would do in your ideal job. Visualize it. *What activities would you do? What do you enjoy doing? What are you passionate about?* Imagine your day. Once you've been on this journey of self-discovery, write your job description and see how your current role and any future jobs you are interested in align with this.

3. List everything you're good at and all your achievements – we don't always celebrate ourselves enough, so track your accomplishments and professional successes. Consider your strengths and the things you enjoy doing and do well.

4. Leave on good terms – if you want a reference or recommendation from your boss, it's important to submit your notice and commit to finishing your last two weeks strong. You can then leave with a clear conscience. Be sure to tell your boss exactly why you're leaving and what you're not happy with, as you never know, they could come back with an offer, and you just might

reconsider. Make sure it's what you want and aligns with your goals and values!

5. Let others know you're looking for a new challenge and ask for recommendations – people can refer jobs to you or refer you to companies that are looking for a new employee based on your capabilities. LinkedIn is an excellent resource for this, as you can update your skills and resume online, making referrals much easier.

Finances are always a concern before quitting your job, so let's discuss these in more detail next. Always ensure you're in good financial standing before you quit your job, and while we've touched on these a little already, let's consider how you can be more financially secure.

7 Tips to Secure Your Finances Before You Quit Your Job

If you ensure your finances are secure before you quit your job, it can make setting up in business so much easier. Quitting your job is a big step, especially if you're starting up in business, as you go from getting a pay check every month to not knowing where your next income is coming from. Nothing is guaranteed!

Your finances are important, so if you want to ensure your financial security, do the following:

1. Understand your current financial situation. Take a full inventory of your money, your fixed spending, and other regular expenses.
2. Make sure you have at least 3-6 months of money saved to pay your living expenses. Let's be clear. I'm talking about fixed bills here. Not all the 'nice to have's. These are restaurants, clothing you don't have to buy, etc. I'm only referring to the monthly payments you will have to make. For most people, this is around $5,000/month. Concentrating on finding a new job or starting your business is difficult if you constantly worry about money.
3. Make an attempt to reduce the debt you have and keep it at a manageable level. See what credit cards you can pay off before you leave —any outstanding car payments, etc. Getting rid of debt before you go will make it mentally easier for you while you are building your business.
4. Be strict regarding budgeting and keep your expenses as low as possible. Look for ways to make cuts in your spending. Always stick to your budget. Don't be afraid to make changes, such as shopping in more reasonably priced stores, buying cheaper items, or cutting out the shopping completely if not 100% necessary. At least just for the time being.

5. Saving is a priority, so remember this. You must ensure you have enough for your future, including retirement. Make sure you have a savings plan, even if this means dipping into your savings plan right now. You will recoup it later.
6. Are there any other ways to make money? Maybe you could freelance a few hours per week to build up your savings or can set up alternative income streams to help you bring in some extra $$$. The quicker, the better!
7. Put a plan in place. While you're setting up a business, it's important to set goals and think about what you will do for money if things don't go as planned. Keeping your eyes open for opportunities is useful and reduces stress if you have a backup plan.

It can be tempting to quit your job and make a move to an online business, but financial situations can make this a scary prospect. If you start doing some freelance work before you quit, it will give you some idea of what's out there for you to do – it helps you assess the gap in the market. The economy and job market are not certain and can be unpredictable. Ensuring your finances are in good order helps you go all-in with your business because you don't have to worry. However, you don't want your savings to disappear before you start making money with your business. There's no shame in having a safety net, especially if you have responsibilities (like I do).

How to Manage Your Income and Expenditure Effectively

Budgeting is an important part of starting a business. To budget well, you need to manage your income and expenditure effectively. Here's how:

- Detail your net income – this is your take-home pay.
- List your monthly expenses. Don't forget to detail your loans or credit card payments, mortgage, insurance, utilities, food, household goods, shopping, and subscriptions such as your internet, cellphone, or streaming services. You must include those costs if you have a vehicle or travel a lot. This means regular monthly expenses (like gym memberships, travel, entertainment, etc.).
- When you have a list, identify fixed expenses and variable ones. Variable means that the amount changes month to month but fixed means the amounts are the same every month. For your variables, you may want to come up with an average so you can know the amount to come up each month.

- Make a plan – look at your income and expenditure and see if there are any ways for you to increase your savings. Set financial goals based on what you want to achieve in line with that but ensure they're realistic.

- When you're budgeting, it's suggested you use the 50/30/20 rule, which means you use 50% of your income for your essential payments (your needs). 30% of your income can be used for wants (non-essential spending), although you'll need to tweak this and use less if you want to tighten your budget. 20% of your income should then go to your savings or paying down your debt. This can also help you figure out your salary goals; this way, you know what you want to earn when you start your online business.

Your Budget

Start creating your budget today using my simple budgeting template. All you have to do is complete it. You can even tweak it to include the things you want to include:

Remember...

> *"Financial peace isn't the acquisition of stuff. It's learning to live on less than you make, so you*

can give money back and have money to invest.
You can't win until you do this." ~ Dave Ramsey

Money is important because we need it to survive. This is extremely important if you're a business owner, as living paycheck to paycheck is stressful, but there are other skills you need if you want to run an online business and crush your financial worries. As well as being financially stable, it's also important that you manage your time effectively. We've dedicated a whole chapter to this next.

OK, if you are enjoying my book and getting some really great ideas so far, **please take 5 minutes of your time right now and head over to Amazon to leave me your honest feedback.** I'm counting on it as a new author to help me spread the word about my book. Still, your feedback will also help many other women looking for this information so they, too, can break free of the 9-5 and start living the life they have always dreamt of, so don't hesitate, take 2 minutes right now and leave me your feedback, even if it's just a 5-start rating, that already goes a long way.

5

IMPROVING YOUR TIME MANAGEMENT SKILLS

*Y*ou'll constantly hear people talk about time management and its importance. While we'd all like to master this skill, it's not always easy. When you're running your business, time management is more important than ever because you'll need to do more, and it will feel like you are always running out of time. This chapter focuses on effective strategies to do just that.

Time management is basically organizing and planning your time effectively so that you can get more done in your available time. This means controlling the time you spend on each task while ensuring it's completed to a high quality. Good time management means you ultimately get more done in less time and still meet your deadlines. You want to smash that to-do list!

We'll explore the reasons why time management is an essential skill for business owners. Without it, success will be just a dream. We'll also discuss ways to increase your productivity, so you can get things done, even if you're pressed for time.

Time management is a relatively simple skill to master, and once you've it down, you'll wonder why it took you this long in the first place. Your time is precious and should be valued highly because when you're a business owner, every moment you spend working should make you money and add a huge value to the business.

Let's talk about why time is of the essence!

Why Is Time Management So Important for Business Owners?

Time is precious. I know that I certainly don't want to spend every waking hour working, which is an easy trap to fall into when you run your own business. When I first started working online, I wanted as much flexibility as possible, but I also wanted to spend more time with my family. As I get older, I become acutely aware of how little time I have to accomplish everything I want. Don't get me wrong; I'm not saying I'm running out of time; I am saying I don't want to waste a second more than I have to. This is why being aware of where your time goes is so important:

- You can accomplish more in less time if you manage it well.
- You can make better decisions and prioritize tasks based on importance by making the most of your time.
- Much less stress, as you'll know what you're doing and when you're doing it. Your mental health impacts your business, so keeping stress down to a minimum will create a more harmonious workplace/home office with more motivated staff/you.
- You utilize your time, which builds efficiency, and allows you to move the needle forward consistently.
- You'll have more time for growth. If you manage your time effectively, you'll find that you have more time to work ON your business and not just in it. You'll have to learn new skills, but if you're managing your time well, there's no reason why you can't grow your skills whilst also pushing for the growth of your business.
- The quality of the work you produce will also improve. You will have more time to focus on specific tasks, so the turn-around and quality will improve as your confidence grows.
- Your business will get better results, partly because the work becomes enjoyable, increasing your motivation.

When running your own business, you're always expected to be your best every day. Prioritizing your tasks, increasing productivity, and making good progress, provide your business with what it needs to survive and thrive.

Imagine this...

You're running your own business, and you only have to work for a few hours each day to accomplish your goals. This gives you more time with your family, and a shorter working day and causes you less stress. As you've completed your goals, you're still earning the income you desire as well...

Sounds like a dream, *right?* Well, there's no reason why you can't do this, and you'll soon reap the results by seeing the positive impact it has on you and your business.

Imagine your life when you master these crucial skills. Just sit and visualize for a moment... *How does it feel?*

It's Time to Get Way Better at Time Management

We've talked about the importance of time management, but we haven't really discussed how you could improve your skills. The key to this, ultimately, is planning.

1. Figure out when you're most productive – we all have different times of the day in which we're more productive. Some people work best at night, while others find that they

function best if they get up an hour early. Just ensure you have time to rest and refresh to avoid burnout.

2. Prioritize your work by doing the urgent work first, then the important one, followed by anything else that still needs to get done, but it's not going to kill you if you don't complete it today. This ensures you're working in a logical and efficient way.

3. Plan your work by scheduling your work tasks, meetings, and goals in your calendar. Block off your deadlines and tick off your to-do list as you go. It's important to plan the month, then break it down into weeks and then into days, hours, and minutes. Be as specific as possible. This keeps you motivated because you are seeing your progress day by day. Don't tell yourself you will spend 10-15 hours per week. You won't. Plan each hour of each day and break it down into half-hour increments. Know exactly where your time is going. This is my *trick* to staying mega-motivated.

4. Focus on one thing at a time. Many people talk about their ability to multitask. However, this is NOT productive at all. It's a lie. Don't believe it. Focusing on one thing at a time can help increase your focus and productivity, and you will finish your tasks quicker with zero mistakes. When you

multitask, you allow room for error. Avoid it if you can.

5. Turn off your notifications, and ignore your social media and emails (unless it's your scheduled time), which means you will actually need to schedule the time to allow yourself to scroll through your social media apps. I allow myself half-hour increments every 4 hours. This keeps me focused on the task at hand and minimizes distractions. I can get distracted quickly, so I need to be really diligent with this. Most people have difficulty staying on task because social media is addictive. If you don't control it, it will control you. You have to be in charge. You make the decision when you allow the distraction. It's ok to allow it as long as it's limited.

6. Ensure you're getting rest. Rework your schedule so that you can get enough time to sleep. If this means going to bed one hour earlier, so be it. Burnout is proven to happen quicker if you are not sleeping enough. It's a good idea to also allow breaks throughout the day. During your lunch break, try going for a walk, hugging a tree (I do it), joining a class, or just sitting quietly for a bit (meditate, get quiet). You will see a massive shift in your mental and emotional health, which will directly affect your energy levels.

7. Do what works for you. Ensure that you stick to the best when planning your time and using different strategies or tools. As you are experimenting with different strategies, it will take time in the beginning. When you find what works, be consistent and make it your daily habit. Remember, habits take 21 days to stick, so keep it going until it becomes second nature.
8. We've spoken a lot about focus, which is great; however, pay attention to the things that distract you from your work, so you know exactly what you need to limit or avoid

While time management is extremely important, it's equally crucial to increase your productivity simultaneously. Let's talk about some powerful productivity strategies; even when you're pressed for time, you can apply these.

Powerful Strategies to Increase Your Productivity During a Time Crunch

When we talk about productivity, we refer to the volume of work you produce, its quality, and its efficiency. Being productive ultimately means increasing your work output without sacrificing quality – basically, you're doing more work but spending the same amount of time.

When you say it aloud, it sounds impossible – *how can we possibly do more?* But there are some ways you can increase your productivity, even if your time is limited.

There are five key ways to improve efficiency:

1. Ensure you have clarity. There's nothing worse when you have a task to complete, but you're not clear. You waste a lot of time figuring out what to do and spend even more time worrying that you are doing it wrong. If you're completing a task, simply ask questions and ensure clarity before you begin. A five-minute discussion can save you hours of worry and frustration. Then concentrate your energy and efforts on getting it done!

2. Speed up your processes by developing templates and checklists. If you have a template, you simply have to add in information then it's done. Automate tasks as much as possible. This works with reports, emails, financial information, presentations, etc. It will make your life a whole lot easier!

3. Create a schedule and list of all tasks, and use time-blocking techniques to manage your time better.

4. Build your efficiency by determining how long each task will take. Consider how it

could be done faster without losing quality (this is where templates and checklists can help).

5. Increase your focus. If you are distracted or find that you procrastinate easily, it's likely that you are lacking focus. Pay attention to the things that distract you or grab your attention and take action to eliminate them. For example, on social media, turn off your notifications and keep your phone silent while completing other jobs. Eliminate anything that will take you away from completing the task. Be strict with yourself at the beginning until you build this habit and it becomes a part of your routine.

Ready to Get Clock-Friendly?

Are you ready to try this on and become more productive throughout the day? If so, you can use this activity to tweak your schedule. You will ensure you're productive all day, even when your energy levels are low.

1. Track your activities over the next 24 hours (simply it down on paper – when you work, read, eat, feel hungry, exercise, or take a break).
2. It's important that you're honest with yourself.

3. Consider your activities and mark when;
4. You have the most fun
5. You are most productive (Rate between 1-5. 1 being least productive and 5 being highly productive).
6. Your energy levels are high
7. Your energy levels are low
8. Evaluate when you are more productive and when your energy levels are high, so you can start doing the most challenging tasks. So, if you are more productive between 7 and 11 in the morning, schedule the tasks you find challenging.
9. Look at what tasks you have the most fun doing and when your energy levels are low. Start scheduling your fun tasks here when your energy levels are low. So, if you find social media fun and it's part of your job to use it, schedule it when your energy is low! If it's not part of your job, schedule a half hour 3 times per day or reserve it until you are done with your work at the end of the day.

If you use this activity to tweak your schedule, you will be much more productive throughout the day. You're basically calibrating your internal clock to match your activities so that you can utilize your productivity. You'll also be able to match the tasks you complete to your energy levels, encouraging you to work more effectively and efficiently. It will also help you to build consistency.

Having this level of awareness of what works best for you and when you are at your peak makes a difference!

SECTION III

Assessing the Skills, You Already Have

6

TAKING STOCK OF ALL YOUR SKILLS

ou have a ton of experience which means you have a ton of skills you have been learning and using throughout your career, be it long or short. Take a moment to reflect and review them. Write them all down. It will be eye-opening. You will realize that we have many skills you didn't even realize you had. Also, consider what we can't do and what it will take to up-skill. Once you are more clear, you can make a decision whether you will learn the skill you need or outsource that part of the project. I do this a lot. I take stock not only of my skills but also of what I enjoy doing and outsource everything that I don't like to do or don't know how to do. Let's be real. I can't be a Jill of all trades. I have my talents, but there is a limit. You don't have to break the bank to outsource, either. There are many relatively inexpensive professionals out there who are really good at what they do. Will will address this a little further down.

Understanding what you are good at boosts your self-confidence. When you start off in business, you need to be confident in the services you offer and show that YOU are the subject-matter expert (a SME) – the person they should choose to work with. Your target audience doesn't want someone who 'thinks' they can give them what they need; they want someone who 'knows' they can. Many people go into business without that spark of confidence because they think they are taking a risk and doubting themselves, and maybe they are taking a small risk, but if you just keep going, there is a good chance you will succeed. Those who fail to stop 2 centimeters (1 inch) from the finish line. They simply don't believe in themselves enough. To be a business owner and sell your products and services, you must have faith that you will make it – if you don't, your customers will sense it and choose someone else instead of you.

This chapter is extremely important because you'll learn to increase your self-worth. You'll also have the opportunity to explore your strengths and learn powerful strategies to help you express your full potential.

> "I was once afraid of people saying, 'Who does she think she is?' Now I have the courage to stand and say, 'This is who I am. I am Oprah."

~ Oprah Winfrey

Let's begin by talking about you because you are worthy (even if you don't always see it)!

You Are Worthy

I just want you to know that it's okay to NOT be good at everything... I'm not. I'm not selling myself short; I have plenty of strengths, skills, and qualities. I just know what they are and where I'm limited, and that's the trick, to know what you're good at and what you should be outsourcing rather than beating yourself up over it. That's called making smart business decisions.

Your feelings, thoughts, and beliefs about yourself will determine your self-worth. If you tend to focus on the positives, you'll have a higher level of self-esteem; if you mostly see only the negatives, your self-esteem will dip. Self-worth is more about recognizing your value. It's about taking the things you're both good at and not-so-good at, and knowing that you're greater than the sum of all of those things. You know you deserve respect because you're a good person, and you respect yourself first. The more confident you become as a business owner, the more confident you will be, period. The more confidence you have, the more value you see in yourself and the more respect you command. You will need that because sometimes you must say 'no' and simply walk away. We will touch on that a bit later.

Remember, you are an expert; act like it, and it will begin to feel real. I promise.

To begin recognizing your self-worth in business, start with a little self-evaluation.

A self-evaluation allows you to check out your performance in an honest and objective way. If done properly, it can be really effective. You get to look at your achievements, assess your performance, and think about ways to improve. You will then be able to set goals for yourself to improve your career and competence.

To complete a powerful self-evaluation:

- Track and map your progress from your previous review (if you've had one). If you didn't, you should keep track of this information as soon as possible and update it regularly.
- Be honest when reflecting on the goals you have or haven't achieved. It's important to accept that not everything works out, but then come up with a plan to help you get organized and start completing small weekly goals.
- Spotlight yourself, but don't limit it to only your work. Look beyond your job and consider anything you've done that helps the community, such as your volunteering work.

Think about what you're really good at and what you want or need to improve.

- Be as specific as possible. If you completed a task that was a complete success, don't just say it; talk about *how* you did it and *what* you learned from the experience.
- Don't be afraid to ask for feedback from others. Ask managers, colleagues, friends, and family if you believe they can be objective and have your best at heart. Only ask those who want to see you succeed. This is imperative.
- Don't just self-evaluate in 5 minutes. Set aside an hour and really think about the task at hand. Relax! This isn't an interrogation. Regular self-evaluations help you succeed in life! Period.

Be honest with yourself when you do this exercise. When I did it, I found out I never spotlighted my achievements. Not really. I mentioned them in passing but never truly celebrated any of them. I bet any money; you don't either. Why? Because women generally never do. After this self-evaluation, I started to celebrate all the little wins as much as the big ones. It's important to celebrate them all. It's really motivating, and it builds our self-esteem.

You've worked hard and reap the rewards because you deserve it. You should find that the more you achieve and celebrate, the more motivated you are to achieve. Your confidence will grow, and you will flourish. Guaranteed.

Exploring Your Strengths

Let's be real. You have a ton of different strengths. Whether you are aware of them all or not, believe me, they are there. Know them inside out because you can play to those strengths as a business owner. Some of the skills you need will be hard skills, such as using a computer. This is a hard skill. Our hard skills are easier to identify. Next, you will need to drill down on your soft skills.

Your soft skills demonstrate your ability to communicate with others, lead people, and think critically or analytically. Let's say your hard skill is using computers and computer software, but your soft skills allow you to think and respond to your emails and then communicate your response accordingly. Skills such as adapting to changes and challenges, being a team player, or resolving difficult situations are all part of the 'soft skill family,' and most of these cannot be measured on paper. Generally, we learn these skills from experience. Our strengths are not always learned in the classroom; as business owners, resilience and mental toughness are just two skills we need to master.

Consider how your soft skills allow you to do your job and:

- Identify your hard skills and soft skills. Write them down in two separate columns.
- Think about how your soft skills have helped you do your job well.
- Consider what soft skills you'd like to develop further.
- Ask others what they believe your strengths are, but have them explain why they think that.

Having self-confidence is a critical part of running your own business. If you have confidence, you're more likely to take risks, try new things, and seize opportunities that show up in front of you. You will go for the things you really want in life instead of shying away from them. That's the goal.

Passion and belief that you have a great business idea that will work are key. You must believe in it and be able to talk about it with potential clients. Your passion and belief will sell them on it, and that's what selling is all about. Passion + Belief = Results. No one will buy unless they are confident in you and your ability to deliver on your promise.

Remember, the first time a customer buys a product or service from you, they are taking a risk. You mitigate this risk by providing them with a solution that works for them and feeling confident that you did a kick-ass job. When you've delivered an awesome solution and gotten positive feedback from clients, it validates your decision to go into business, boosting the overall image you hold of yourself. It's all connected!

Self-doubt is not conducive to your success. *If you don't believe that you can do it, how can you expect others to believe in you?* I know this is a bit backward because when you're first starting, you doubt everything. Ever heard of the saying, "fake it till you make it"? Well, this is kind of like that. You don't necessarily fake it, but you do sort of put the horse before the carriage. You believe first, and everything will fall into place. So it's important that when you're first starting out, you're providing something you believe in and are passionate about. It's much easier to market something you love and believe in than something you don't. I'm speaking from experience here. I tried it both ways. I failed at one. Want to guess which one? That's right, the one that I didn't believe in. I had no drive, no motivation even to start, and when I finally started to put the product together, it sucked so bad. I was too embarrassed to put it out on the market, but I did it anyway, and guess what? No one bought it. I should have known better. Now I do.

Powerful Strategies to Ensure You Reach Your Full Potential

You'll have heard others talk about reaching their 'full potential,' but what does it really mean? It's something I've personally been skeptical about; *I mean, does*

KARINA G. SANCHEZ

anyone really reach their full potential? Once I achieve a goal, I always set another, so I continuously aim to grow. I always thought I'd be done if I reached my full potential, but I've realized that reaching your full potential doesn't mean you'll stop. Before we look into the powerful strategies I'm disclosing, let's confirm what the term means, 'full potential.'

I always thought that reaching your full potential meant you became the best you could ever be. For example, if you wanted to become a doctor and you did, but then your goal was to have a good reputation and start your private practice, once you reached that goal (with no further promotion possibilities), that's it. But when I explored the idea of meeting your full potential, I realized that's not the end. Full potential means being the best you can be, but the best you can be today doesn't mean it's the best you can be tomorrow...

Reaching our full potential right now means learning all the skills, qualities, qualifications, and experience you need right now and becoming the best at those. Next year, when your business needs are different, and you have grown further, you will be reaching and starving for new levels of success. For example, with their practices, doctors could find themselves giving lectures, writing papers or books, and conducting research in their field. They could even adopt new and innovative methods or practices to improve healthcare.

That means that reaching your full potential is not limiting; it's limitless, strengthening the need for constant self-evaluation.

To keep reaching your full potential:

1. Complete a self-evaluation periodically as needed.
2. Develop a growth mindset, which means you will continue to grow without stopping. Focus on effort rather than the outcome. This means you are willing to embrace challenges and change. You will not shy away from them.
3. Take time to reflect and act. Reflect on your self-evaluation (or tasks you've completed during the past week or 24 hours), and then create a goal to build momentum. Getting someone to hold you accountable for your goals is also a good idea to ensure you see them through. Accountability partners make a world of difference. You can help each other stay honest and on task. Find someone that is currently setting goals for themselves and see if you can help each other get to the finish line each week.
4. Focus on the bigger why. You have to take many small steps to get to the bigger goal. The bigger goal is ultimately what you're aiming for, but the smaller steps are what get

you there. Keep reminding yourself of the bigger picture, but focus on the end goal. Use it to drive your progress. You're doing these small tasks so you can achieve the big goal. Just put one foot in front of the other and see things happen.

5. Manage your time effectively. I've provided you with strategies to improve your time management skills in chapter 5, so don't use 'I don't have enough time' as an excuse. To reach your full potential, master time management.

6. Develop your goals. Even when you achieve your goal, reflect and consider what you would do differently or what strengths and skills you've used to do it. Use visualization techniques to imagine how you would approach this differently in an improved way. I always solve the problem in *my mind first*. I see the problem first, imagine different solutions with different outcomes, and then sleep on it. The next day, the solution becomes clearer. I only act once I feel that the solution presented is the right way to go.

7. Remember that the bigger your aspirations, the more time it will take to get there. People fail because they are impatient. They think this is a get-rich-quick scheme, and it's not. Anything valuable takes time to build. Setting a roadmap you can follow will make a

difference in your motivation. I always set 1-year, 2-year, 3-year, 4-year, and 5-year goals. I want to ground myself in realistic expectations for my business. I researched to see what others with similar goals have accomplished and how long it took them to reach each milestone. Then I know what I can expect, and it becomes achievable.

8. Be disciplined. For example, if you're following time management strategies and are time-blocking, don't stray from your path; stick to it. Make sure you have some time scheduled for reflection. I reflect weekly. I think about what I need to keep doing, stop doing, or change. I also reflect on how I showed up that week. How were my energy, my enthusiasm, motivation, and passion? Am I still on track with all of them? If not, why? What's changed? Keep a diary. It will be amazing how much you have grown in a year.

9. Learn from what others have done. If someone has already done something you want to do, learn from their success and mistakes. Don't reinvent the wheel if you don't have it. In fact, it will slow you down.

10. Mistakes have already been mentioned, but it's important that you view failures and mistakes as learnings, not setbacks. Failure isn't fun, but beating yourself up about it is

not proactive; in fact, it can have a negative impact on how you perform. Here is the truth about failure. It's NOT real. It doesn't exist. It's a construct that only exists in your mind. The only time you will fail is if YOU stop moving forward, and that's impossible. Own your mistakes, reflect on them, and be compassionate with yourself. The sooner you pick yourself up, the easier it is to get back on the saddle again. Everyone gets set back from time to time, but learning to deal with it will make you so resilient that nothing will bring you down. Trust me, I have had so many setbacks, and I'm still here. I'm pretty sure I will continue to get set back, and I will continue to move forward. As long as I don't stop, I win.

11. Take time for yourself. It's impossible to reach your goals if you're not taking time to recharge. Not everything in life is about work, even if you love it. You must walk away from time to time to continue loving it. This is a marathon, not a sprint. You are here for the long run. Ensure you're getting enough sleep and taking time to relax. Rest releases happy hormones. They help you stay in joy, and joy is where everything happens. Things just flow easier when you are experiencing joy. I call it my *getting back to joy* time.

Remember, your goals will change over time, so keep evaluating and assessing your skills, and keep working on that growth mindset to keep being the best you can be.

You are awesome now, and you will be even more awesome tomorrow!

Self-Assessment

You can take a few steps to assess where you are right now. When you know, you can put a plan in place to ensure you achieve your dreams.

1. You've already started considering your existing skills and talents. You don't necessarily need to acquire more skills, but you can improve your skills and talents. Think about those that are most relevant or in demand for your business. *Are there any you need to update, upgrade, or refresh? Maybe you know the basics but can take your skills or talents to the next level.*

2. Change how you feel about failure. Call them setbacks instead, and don't let them hold you back.

- Think of your most recent setback.
- Note down what went wrong.
- Visualize how this could've worked better (in an ideal situation).
- Reflect – *are there any skills you need or need to improve for this to work better next time?*
- Use this setback as motivation – you'll do it right next time!
- Follow these steps every time you experience a setback.

3. Practice discipline. Set your schedule and stick to it as closely as possible. That doesn't mean you shouldn't

have flexibility, but make sure you're not simply avoiding work tasks and ensuring you're working productively – get things done. Keep track of your progress and productivity by checking things off your to-do list. If you're struggling with accountability, collaborate with someone who will hold you accountable. This could be a coach, a colleague, or even a family member (provided they can motivate you).

While starting a business may be something you've thought about, *do you have a business idea in mind? Do you know what you want to do? Do you know what niche you should be looking into?*

Don't worry if you haven't quite figured that out yet; in the next chapter, we'll focus on niching and why this is so important for your online business to succeed.

7

HOW TO DEFINE YOUR NICHE

*Y*our niche is basically your thing! It's the 'thing' that you're good at, and this 'thing' also shapes your business, just like it shaped mine.

To define this more clearly, your niche is your specialty area. For example, a person who works in a leading financial corporation may have found that their niche lies in advising people on how to invest their money or organize their finances. This means that their ideal dream job is in finance because they're suitably qualified, talented, and/or experienced in that topic and can help others achieve their financial goals. In essence, they are helping others succeed and can make money from focusing on this particular niche.

Many businesses start without being clear about their niche, but your niche is the most important part you need to get clear about if you want to run your business efficiently and actually make money. Most people make the mistake of casting a very wide net. They try to appeal to everyone and end up appealing to no one. That's a mistake that can cost you time and money. In this chapter, we'll explore how to discover your niche. We'll also talk about your audience, and I'll provide you with some important tips to help you find your target audience as well as learn how to ask qualifying questions to help you identify who your potential customers are - your ideal clients.

> *"Sometimes your limitations become your strengths. It forces you to create your own niche."*
> *~ Dennis DeYoung*

The Benefits of Finding Your Niche

There are many reasons why it's beneficial to find your niche, but some business owners, especially in the early stages of entrepreneurship, don't realize just how important it is.

Let's explore 5 key benefits of finding your niche so you are talking to the right people rather than just talking. Having a clear niche:

- Helps you create the right brand marketing –
  it helps when you know who you are talking
  to so that you can align all your marketing.
  That includes the words that come out of
  your mouth, your social media channels, and

any content that you put together. This way, your clients and potential clients know exactly what services you offer and how you can help them succeed. Don't worry; you are not cutting anyone out. You are speaking to the exact audience you need to be speaking to and no one else.

- Ensures you can establish a loyal client base – once you have helped one person and have done an amazing job, the word will spread quickly. You will become a subject-matter expert in that 'one' thing, and everyone will come to you because they will know that no one else does it better than you. Wow! What a place to be in. You will build a list of long-term, returning, clients that will happily refer you to others.

- Reduces marketing costs – if you know who your customers are, you can use targeted marketing which will save you money. Rather than marketing to everyone, targeted marketing means you focus on your ideal clients, and it focuses or shows up only to people who fall within your required demographics and psychographics. In essence, you will be spending less money and will see better results.

- It's an opportunity to stand out from the competition – if you show your business as being different from others, it means you strengthen your position as an expert, and rather than being lost in a mass market, your niche will decrease or even remove competition. Makes life way easier for you. Less competition means you can service more people, which means you will make more money.

- It will increase your profit – developing your niche that has little competition will allow you to charge higher rates for your products and services. Your clients will be willing to pay higher fees because they know that they can't get that service anywhere else, and won't want to change it. When you have a good idea, have a clear niche, and market your business effectively, it will become highly lucrative.

Finding Your Niche

Finding your niche is easier for some but not for others. In business, it's important to focus on what you're good at, as many people want a product or service that is of high quality and packed with value. If you're not sure what your niche is yet, follow the steps below to clarify it:

1. What are your interests and passions? Make a list of 10-15 skills that you have or are good

at. Do a brain dump. Don't judge it; just put it on paper.

2. What problems can you solve? Think about what you're good at, and consider how you like to 'help' others. We purchase products and services when we have a need, so this question involves considering why there is a 'need' for the product or service you're selling and writing this down.

3. Who are your competitors, and how are you different? It's really important that you know who your competitors are. You should also consider how you are different from your competition, so do some research. Knowing your competitors can help you figure out how you can stand out from the crow and offer something unique.

4. How will you make money, and how much will you make? When you have determined your niche, or at least narrowed it down, you need to consider how much money you can make from this idea. You should have an idea of your price point, so make a note of that.

5. Test your idea! You now have all the information you need to choose your niche. You should be clear on your idea and recognize who your customers are and how you can reach them. It's time to see if your idea is viable, so you should set up a landing page, for pre-sales. You should then be

marketing your idea – making sure you target the right people and drive them to this page. If you don't make sales, but drive plenty of people in that direction, your idea or offer has not failed; it's likely it just needs tweaking. Try to look out for possible issues that are preventing your clients from taking action.

Figuring Out Your Audience

In business, we all have an audience, but it's important that you're more specific than this as you need a specific audience that your product or service appeals to. You can target your audience by considering age, gender, income levels, interests, or locations. There are other factors to consider, too – for example, you can target people based on their careers and whether they are parents or not.

Your target audience depends on the product and service you're selling, and they should be the people who are most likely to buy it. When you know your niche and have clarity of who you're selling to, it makes running your business so much easier and so much more successful.

For some people, their target audience is quite broad; however, being able to define and segment your audience effectively can allow you to have a much clearer message.

For example, a shoe store may aim to sell shoes to

men, women, and children of all ages, so their audience is broad. If the shoe store decided to specialize in a specific shoe, such as walking boots, the audience is the people who are interested in walking. Some shoe stores may niche further and specifically supply children's walking boots, with a fitting service to ensure they get the right boot for comfort reasons. The fitting service offers that extra value which could be a unique selling point to bring in customers – if a child is going to be hiking, it's likely that whoever is buying them the boots will want them to be as comfortable as possible.

5 Tip Tips to Finding Your Target Audience

If you want to find your target audience, there are some things you need to know to ensure you're attracting the attention of the right people.

1. Analyze your customer base – this means exploring who already buys similar products and services and then looking at them in more detail – how old are they? What are their interests? Where do they live? Many businesses learn this information by distributing surveys or polls or by engaging on social media.

2. Complete market research – this means looking at your industry by reviewing trends and by looking for gaps in the market. You should be asking yourself if there are any

gaps in the market your business can fill. What do other businesses offer, and how are your products or services different?

3. Look at competitors- it's important you look closely at your competitors. Pay attention to where your competitors are focusing their efforts. Of course, you need to think about how your products are different from that of your competitors too – so ask how you can make your products or services unique and who they are focusing on exactly.

4. Define your target audience and create an avatar of your ideal client – then create qualifying questions to find the needle in the haystack (we learn how to do this in the next section). Then, we drill down to find your exact target audience. One way to do this is to create a person or an avatar that highlights the way your client can be segmented. For example, consider a range of demographics, psychographics, behaviors, and personalities. There is so much you can learn if you know the customer you are serving.

5. Keep revising – you must continuously look at and revise your strategy. As your business develops, you'll gather more client information, and you'll be able to tweak your ideal client. If the market changes, you can continuously optimize your target audiences

to ensure your business achieves the best results.

Target Audience – The Qualifying Questions

The idea of having a target audience is to encourage the right people to buy your product or service. To be the right person, the product or service you provide has to be something they need or want. In question 4 of the last section, I mentioned the term 'qualifying questions,' so now, I want to explain what I mean…

Basically, qualifying questions will indicate if a person is likely to become a paying client or not. I've provided a list of questions below for YOU to answer about your target audience. When you've answered these questions, you can start to put a picture together of who your client is. This will help you market what you're selling, effectively.

There are 9 questions for you to answer:

• What are your ideal customer demographics?

Demographics include information about their marital status, their gender, and their age group. You may also consider where your ideal clients live, but if you're an online business, you need to consider what countries or places you'll provide your products or services in. This is often a key demographic for a person who has a physical business, such as a store.

- What career or industry do they work in?

Sometimes, your client's career or the industry they work in may be relevant to your business, but this isn't the case for every business model, or maybe the industry itself is relevant to your product or service. If you have an idea of their career or industry, it can allow you to consider other things such as promotional opportunities, income, items they may need or want for work purposes, as well as their level of education.

- What is their income like?

This can depend on your target audience's career, but it can also depend on whether it's a single or a double-income household. Income is important for obvious reasons. It tells us how much your target audience can spend on your product/service. If they are in the low-income bracket, chances are, they will not be able to spend $10,000 on a training program, so you'll need to ensure that your products/services are affordable for your target audience, or you may consider having a lower and a higher-end product available.

- What hobbies do they enjoy?

Think about the audience as one person. What do they like to do? How do they spend their free time? What are they passionate about? If you're talking about people who have families – consider things they may do as part of that role.

- If your client wants to buy something, how do they get their information or communicate their interest?

Advertising used to be simple – meaning it took place on billboards, in shop windows, in newspapers or magazines, or on TV, but now, marketing is largely online. Most people are on social media, receive emails, and read both online articles and blogs, so it's worth reaching out via the right method. You need to check that your ideal client uses the platform you use for marketing – for example, if you cater to adults over 80, not many may be on social media, nor will they engage with online marketing. You also need to know their preferred method of communication, and when they are likely to respond to something you're selling, so you know how to reach them.

- How does your ideal client think?

This doesn't mean you have to be psychic exactly, but you have to put yourself in their shoes and imagine what they're thinking about, worrying about. What keeps them up at night? You can actually do some customer research on this on Quora, Reddit, or even YouTube. Consider their personality, values, their lifestyle, behavior, beliefs, and attitudes. What makes them tick, and what doesn't?

- What and who is important to your ideal client?

People tend to buy based on what's important to them. It's an emotional gut reaction, so find out *what* is important to them and *who* is important to them. For instance, for some people, their family is important, or money, their career, or even their lifestyle. Their partner could even influence their buying decisions. Figure out who's the decision maker and speak to them. Knowing this will help you strategize and narrow down your niche.

- What challenges does your audience face?

Your products and services *solve a problem* for your target audience, but to solve it, you need to understand it first. For example, if someone lacks time, you may have something to organize their time. Think about how your product or service solves this problem.

- What drives them to buy?

When your client decides to buy something, it's a decision that they are driven by their emotional need. You need to know what influences them, what obstacles are in their way, and what their biggest objections are to buy your service. Remember, an objection is not a 'no'; it's an ask for more information. You simply haven't given them enough of a good reason to buy yet. Refine your approach, answer their questions, and provide them with the solution, you know they need.

Once you've answered these questions, you've basically identified your target audience. This means you can create your ideal client avatar profile. This way, when you're marketing your products and service, you know exactly who your marketing material is aimed at.

Next, it's time to move onto a whole new section, and focus on choosing the right online business for you. Choosing your business is what this is all about. Let's go!

8

CHOOSING YOUR ONLINE
BUSINESS

*O*K, so what's the best online business for you? We know you have to love it, you have to have some skills to do it, and most of all, you want to help others achieve their dreams by solving their problem with your solution. Easy, right? It is, once you know what's the right business for you. In this chapter, we will explore several online business opportunities, so you can identify the one that suits your talents and skills.

It isn't always easy to choose the right online business, as there's so much to consider. The online world is the biggest market available, and the audience is vast, as many people prefer to shop online. For obvious reasons, it's easy and convenient. There are no lineups or crowds, and you can get a much better price without traveling further than your computer. Since the breakout of the last pandemic and then the lockdowns, people have learned to shop online, so no wonder companies like Amazon have quadrupled their sales. If you have been selling online during that time, you made and are still making some good coin. I want you to take part in that.

In this chapter, we're going to talk about your online presence and go through some important steps to help you begin an online business. We're also going to talk about the different online business opportunities that exist out there, so you can recognize, identify, and take advantage of them.

Your Online Presence

Your online presence is really important to how your customers view and perceive you. This is visible in the right way, addressing the right problems. Remember the saying, "people buy from the people they like"? Honestly, if you remember nothing else, remember this. People truly buy from those they like, and how will they discover if they like you? Well, it's how you present yourself online. *What* you say, *how* you say it, and *who* you say it to.

Having an online business is a whole new world; how you present yourself and your business is extremely important as it:

- It helps you build a positive business reputation.

- It allows your audience to get to know you, and once they know you and like you, they will begin to trust you. **Know, like, and trust = sales**
- It helps you find the right customers while giving you access to a wider range of clientele without having to pay expensive marketing fees.

Having a good online marketing and branding strategy will increase your profits dramatically. If you look at marketing ROI (return on investment), it's often higher when the business operates online. That's because this type of marketing is targeted specifically to your audience, but your reach is much larger. Your marketing opportunities are basically limitless. Currently, over 5 billion people are using the internet to make money. 5 billion! Imagine the potential. Amazon alone sells to 156+ customers. Imagine having access to so many people. Now you understand why your online presence is important. Don't stress; I will teach you how.

If your business has a good online presence, it can be found easily by customers because you are extremely visible. To build your online presence, you will use online marketing strategies and web-based channels to get you or your business, and its products and services are seen by potential customers. This means:

- Having a website. This can be simple. Your business/or personal name (if your actual name is your business name, then use that), what you do (service or solution you provide), and who you do it for (your target audience/customer avatar).
- Using Social media channels (Facebook, Instagram, YouTube, TikTok, etc.), I don't suggest using more than two or three if you are proficient or have someone that can handle the social media part for you. It's just too time-consuming, and you will get distracted and pulled away from what's important, and that's building your customer base and making money.
- Building an email list of potential and current clients. You can use a platform like MailChimp, MailerLite, or Kajabi. There are many that are really inexpensive and allow you to collect names in exchange for a free lead magnet (that's generally a document that provides value that you will give them in exchange for their email). I use this, and it works well if you constantly give them something they want.
- Posting a range of high-quality content consistently and regularly to the online platforms you use (website, social media, emails). Again, don't ask for anything yet. For now, you are building trust and giving,

giving, giving. A time will come when you will ask in return for all that you gave, and at that point, they will be willing and receptive.

Online businesses can increase their sustainability, strengthen their brand, and develop their online presence. This is absolutely crucial for the longevity of your brand and, ultimately, your business.

I realized how important it wasn't until I started exploring the different ways to market my business online. I researched the most appropriate social media methods for my business and have been pleasantly surprised by the results. Personally, TikTok and YouTube have proved to be the perfect way for me to increase my presence online, and due to this largely being video content, my clients can get to know me as a person. They relate to my story, so they follow my journey. Remember what we said earlier, if they like me and trust me, they will buy.

It's going back to that philosophy again...

If your clients know, like, and trust you – you will make money.

8 Steps to Starting an Online Business

The online world has made it possible for small business owners to take their services online, adding another source of income. Start-up costs decreased since you can work from home without a massive initial investment, and it's become easier and simpler. The only thing you need to do is learn how. Think of it as growing a new muscle. The initial learning process may take some time, but once you have learned the basics, the rest is just refining and continuing the learning process. The beauty is that you don't have to know it all at the beginning. You take little steps and learn as you go.

Let's take a minute and assess our options…

To help you asses quicker and with better results, I've put together 8 steps to help you start your online business the right way:

1. Start a business that people 'need' – you have done the research. You have an idea of who your ideal customer is. You also have a solution that can help them be successful. It's time to drill down and get even more detail. To do that, you can try the following:

- If you have found someone online who does something similar to what you want to do, do further research into your competition by looking into their business model and seeing what products/services they offer. Assess what they do well and what you can do better or differently.
- Do some keyword research. You can do this on google to find out what keywords people are searching for. On YouTube, for example,

there is software that you can use called
TubeBuddy; it allows you to see what titles
people are searching for to give you an idea
of what topics are in demand. You can do the
same thing on Amazon, just type into the
search window a topic of interest and use
AMZ Suggestion Expander to see what topics
people are interested in. You can also use
Google; just type 'what's trending in business'
and see what happens. You don't need to
overcomplicate this. Do some research and
see what comes up.

- Visiting social media groups or online
  forums to find out what questions people
  have and what problem they need solving –
  see if it's in your wheelhouse.

2. Write a business plan – when you've assessed the
'need' and figured out that your idea has potential,
work on putting together a simplified business plan.
Even if you're starting with no or very little money, you
still need a simple plan so that you get clarity on the
following:

- Your business goals – what you want to
  achieve in year 1, year 2, and year 3. Break it
  down into smaller steps. Starting with these
  smaller objectives will help you get crystal
  clear on what needs to be done now so that
  your 10-year plan has a chance of survival.

- Your business name – think long-term. If it's a service you are providing, you might want to use your name as the business name. Consultants and freelancers do that often. Then, set up your website domain and social media accounts, open a business bank account, and consult with your accountant. Know the benefits of LLCs, sole proprietorships (Canada, UK), incorporations, etc. Ask them to explain the difference so you can choose what's best for you. Taxation is different for each.
- What to do if you encounter any bumps in the road. Consider the problems you may encounter along the way and how you can overcome them, especially if they are financial. Plan ahead.
- Your finances – what you need and how much you expect to earn. You can even include what you need to do to meet your financial goals. Be really realistic here. Remember, getting you off the ground takes a bit of time.
- Your marketing plan – how and where you will market your products/services, how much you will spend on marketing, and your marketing goals and objectives – make sure they're realistic. Marketing can be costly. Set a budget and follow it. Don't get caught up in

the new shiny things because you will overspend.

3. Write good sales copy – what you write when attracting your ideal clients is really important, as it marks the very beginning of the selling process. I recommend you pick up a book or two on copywriting. I love the book, "Copywriting Secrets" by Jim Edwards. Remember that your client always wants to know *'what's in it for them?'*. You need to have a compelling headline that grabs their attention before you describe the problem and provide the solution (that you've figured out in point 1). Next, you need to state your authority by explaining how you're qualified to solve this problem. Once you've been in business for a while, it's a good idea to add testimonials from your happy customers here. Testimonials sell quicker than any other marketing strategy out there. You will finish it all off with a strong guarantee. Whatever that looks like, money back, free offer, etc. Call them to action and create urgency. Maybe your offer is for a limited time, or they get a bonus they can't resist. Whatever it is, make it juicy.

4. You need a landing page – that allows you to capture emails in form of subscribers. There is no need for a stand-alone website anymore. It's more important to grow your customer base and manage it simultaneously. A good platform like MailChimp or MailerLite will do just that. Putting together a landing page is

fairly simple, and most lead capture pages will have existing templates you can use that are so simple you can design a basic landing page yourself. If you need anything extra, you can always go to Fiverr or Upwork and hire a freelancer to design it for you. For $50, someone can design an awesome landing page and integrate it with a lead magnet so that you can start to collect subscribers. You can even have a freelancer put your lead magnet together at a minimum cost. I hired someone on Fiverr, and for $10 got an awesome lead magnet done.

5. Drive traffic to your site by using search engines – the simplest way to get traffic to your site is to optimize your website so it starts showing up on searches. You can use pay-per-click advertising, but you will have to test out your headlines, different keywords, prices, and selling approaches to make this a success. This will instantly direct traffic to your site, and you can monitor your results.

6. Increase your presence and build a positive reputation – the internet includes a wealth of information, and people always use it to find out more information about specific topics. You can become more visible by:

- Giving away free and valuable information, advice, or content, on someone else's social media groups, by getting PR, features, spotlights in online articles, or by speaking at others' events.

- Include links on your posts to social media, blogs, or stories that are valuable, such as a 'send to friend' link or 'share.' Encourage your audience to share your content.
- Be active on social media and in group forms where your target audience hangs out. Just answer questions and network with others; if they find what you say valuable, they'll soon look you up.

7. Embrace email marketing to convert your audience – when people talk about converting their audience, they convert them into paying customers. Building an email list is a great way to stay on the radar of your potential clients, and if you're providing them with value and they like you, they're more likely to become customers. Emails allow you to develop your relationship with them, and the success of your emails and campaigns is easy to measure. Email marketing isn't expensive; it's a cheaper method of marketing because you're emailing warm leads (people who have agreed for you to contact them because they like you or what you're offering). You're providing them with something they've asked for; just make sure you have permission to send them emails first.

8. Use other internet marketing strategies to increase your revenue – internet marketing can be used to

increase sales if you upsell or back-sell. Once a customer has bought from you, they are more likely to buy from you again. You can offer opportunities to buy more from you; for example, when they sign up for a freebie, you can offer them a low-ticket item to accompany the freebie. This should be a product that complements their original purchase. You can also offer coupons so they get cheaper products the next time they buy. It's a way for you to reward them for their loyalty. You can also list further products on your 'Thank You' page.

Now that we've covered the steps of setting up your online business, it's important to explore what opportunities are actually available to you online...

What Online Business Opportunities are Available?

There are so many opportunities and directions you can explore in terms of setting up your online business. Let's explore 15 of the most popular:

1. Affiliate Marketing – this is a way for you to make commissions by referring to another person's product. This works best if you already have a good social media following and a sizeable email list giving you a quick opportunity to earn money without having to invest almost anything at all. You earn money based on the products people buy after

clicking on your affiliate link. Check out Amazon Associates Affiliate Program for more information.

2. Start an online store – you can create the store of your dreams online. Most people enjoy shopping that way, as there are no lineups, wait times or travel associated with traditional shopping. Setting up a store is cheap and easy; it's much more cost-effective than actually opening a physical store that people can visit, and you can sell internationally. This is the way to do it if you have a product you think you'd love to sell. Check out Etsy.com to start getting some ideas.

3. Drop shipping is a retail business where the seller (you) accepts customer orders without keeping stock on hand. When a customer buys a product, your supplier who stores your items (exp., Amazon) ships it directly to your customer. Basically, you never have to buy products in bulk; you never have to handle the product; you just have to process the order through your own online store, which sits inside the Amazon store. You can check out Shopify or Amazon for more information.

4. Publish a book on Amazon – writing a book is a great way to earn money, as you can write in any genre you wish. Simply write your

book on a topic of your choice (or get a writer to do this for you), upload it to Amazon, and you can sell it as an ebook. Other options include using print-on-demand, so if the customer wants a physical book, Amazon will print it and send it to the customer for you. You can also find someone to narrate your book and tap into the audible books business on Audible. This is called self-publishing, and there are many free courses on YouTube on how to self-publish on a budget and start earning royalties on your books.

5. Creating a digital product (including online courses) – you can create and sell digital products, such as craft instructions, recipes, photos, e-books, design templates, PDFs, printables, and courses (including audio or video). You can sell these on your website or on other sites, such as Amazon or SkillShare.

6. Start a YouTube channel – you could create online videos on a specific subject and share your knowledge using Youtube. You can then monetize your account by getting people to subscribe to your account or by password-protecting some of your content that is solely for your paying customers. You could then expand it by promoting snippets of your content on TikTok, which is another platform that can be monetized. The good

thing about videos is that they can be edited, reused, and repurposed.

7. Start a podcast – Just like YouTube, a podcast can be monetized, but it's audio only, and it can be really simple. You can create a podcast using a microphone, your laptop, and recording software (which is obtainable for free). Podcasts are not every day, and podcasters find that they earn money through commercial sponsorship. As the podcast belongs to you, you can even use it as a place to market your products and services, providing you're providing value to your audience.

8. Become a copywriter – copywriters earn a great income. Like all these online business ideas, you can work from anywhere if you can write in a way that grabs the attention of others whilst divulging a fresh marketing message. Copywriting is really in demand for pretty much anyone who sells anything online.

9. Facebook Advertiser – if you've got a talent for attracting clients by marketing on Facebook, this could be the perfect freelance opportunity for you. Businesses pay high rates for those who have mastered the algorithm of Facebook marketing, as this is a lucrative way for them to reach customers, as so many people are active on the platform.

10. Freelance – if you're good at editing, writing, designing, teaching a specific topic, or programming, you can make money through freelance work. While you may start with lower earnings, your reputation on freelance platforms often allows you to work your way to higher-paying jobs quickly.

11. Social Media Marketing Agency – if you're good at marketing on social media and can attract followers, likes, favorites, shares, or retweets, you could become a social media marketing agency. You would work with other businesses to improve their online profiles, increase their reach, and build their brands through marketing. This is very lucrative, and many companies are looking for people who can do it well and increase customer engagement.

12. Internet domain selling – did you know you can sell internet domains? Basically, your research which domain names are selling well, then you buy the high-value domains from cheap online auctions. You then resell them to others. There is an element of risk, as there are no guarantees that the domain names you buy will be bought, but if you are successful at predicting which companies or industries need names, this can be highly lucrative.

13. Trading in Forex – if you like currencies, including foreign exchange, you could benefit from trading in forex. This means you're trading in foreign exchange and currencies. This can be risky if you don't know anything about foreign exchange, so you should familiarize yourself with the market first and foreign exchange first and set yourself up with a broker to ensure you don't get scammed by rogue traders. Forex is the global marketplace for currency. You would then need to decide on a currency that you wanted to trade with and whether you would buy or sell.

14. Travel planning – This could be ideal for you if you love to travel. It involves helping your clients to plan the details of their trip, from transport to accommodation, and including activities and excursions whilst on their trip. Basically, you're planning their whole itinerary. You can run this business from the comfort of your home, but if you travel, this is even better as it allows you to make new connections. Suppose you happen to write a travel blog or have some basic photography skills. In that case, this can work to accompany your travel planning business which will translate into an even greater income opportunity.

15. Graphic design – if you're good at designing logos, posters, or other graphics, you could take a stab at graphic design. Use your existing skills by drawing or creating graphics online while working flexibly. Illustrations bring good money as well. Many online freelancing platforms offer these opportunities. Some are Fiverr, Upwork, Freelancer, etc. We will discuss these a bit later. These can lead to high-paying projects and returning customers.

Now that you have some idea of what different online business opportunities are available, all that's left is for you to decide which one works best for you...

What's Your Perfect Online Business?

After reading the ideas in the above section, brain-dump which online business methods work best for you based on your expertise, skills, and interest.

I'm sure that several will suit you, but try to narrow down your business choice by asking yourself the following questions once you've completed your brainstorming activity:

- Which ideas are you more passionate about?
- Which ideas can you turn into a business and make money?

- Which ideas will help you build a long-term business?
- What is important to you?
- Which business ideas do you feel you should focus on right now?

If this doesn't help you make a decision, it will at least allow you to do more research and see if one of these really resonates with you. List the pros and cons of each, don't rush it. Make the decision that best suits your experience and needs.

In the next section, we will focus on research so that you can plan your business venture appropriately. Many people tell you to 'research' without specifically telling you what you should be researching. That's not the case here. We're going to do this together in chapter 9.

9

DOING YOUR RESEARCH TO FIND YOUR BEST FIT

I've talked about researching quite a lot throughout the previous chapters, and whilst you'll know what research is in theory, it's not always easy to know what you should specifically research or how best to go about it.

If you're starting an online business, research is necessary, so in this chapter, we're going to focus on this by discussing specific strategies to help you conduct thorough market research, whilst also talking about different ways to identify the business that best matches your skills.

Many new business owners fail to do proper market research prior to starting their business, and this is a mistake. Before we go any further, it's important to clarify the importance of market research BEFORE you set up a business.

Let's get started!

The Importance of Market Research BEFORE You Set up Your Business

Market research is extremely important throughout your business journey. It's common for a business to reach its goals and stagnate. Staying current and in need is the goal long-term. It's impossible to tell if your business is viable without conducting your own individual research.

When you're writing your business plan, you'll need to set goals, but *how will you know what goals to set, if you haven't explored your market? In fact, how do you even know that people want your product or service in the first place?*

Completing market research can ensure:

1. Your business idea is viable – in the previous chapter, I talked about ensuring your business idea is viable. This means checking out your competition so you can figure out how your product/service is unique, researching to make sure there is a need for your product/service by communicating with your potential customers, helping you come up with realistic business goals, so you have something to work towards.
2. You're able to secure funding from investors (if applicable) – some businesses require investment, but you can only get the funding if you've done your research as you will be

required to pitch your idea to them first. Your investors want to be certain that you know what you're doing and have done your homework. Your research should focus on the industry itself, what problem your idea solves and how it can be placed in the market, and also, how well you know your competition.

3. You make sound business decisions – it's a fact, we have to make sound business decisions when we're faced with difficulties. If you don't research, you won't know what decisions to make. If you don't have the market information, it's impossible to make an informed decision, especially when you're just starting out. Poor decision-making will put you out of business.

4. Your business starts off successfully and avoids business failures – the market changes and evolves constantly. You'll need to be proactive and aware of your surroundings. If you know the risks, you can anticipate them and come up with a suitable plan of action, reducing the risks greatly. We learned from experience, however, failures are costly and can damage the brand as well as the reputation of the business.

5. You are able to determine new business opportunities – market research is so much more than exploring customer behaviors

and market trends and can lead to new business opportunities. Research can actually lead to growth opportunities for your business. You will find that new revenue streams open up as a result of your research. Finding what people need and filling that need will give you an advantage. Businesses must learn to adapt as the market changes constantly, which may mean tweaking your business model for the greater good. Looking at the market can bring new opportunities to light.

Market Research Strategies

Market research is used in new and current businesses, to test out new products or services, or to collect information from your target market (audience) to discover what they 'need'. There are many different types of market research, including:

1. Interviews – an in-person interview involves meeting with your client face-to-face, either online or via video conference. This means that the business can interview people to ask them a series of simple questions. The data is collected and published so that businesses can look at the results and any relevant comments before making a business decision. You can conduct your own interviews to

gather information to help you move forward.

2. Online research – marketing online is proving more and more effective, as more and more people are spending time online. Data can be collected by asking a single question, creating a poll or survey, or inviting a person to leave feedback via a link. If they've just bought a product or service from your business, they are more open to leaving you feedback or a review.

3. Focus groups – with this method, people attending a focus group can provide their opinions and perceptions regarding a product/service and provide feedback. The feedback is often more detailed and specific in comparison to a yes/no question.

4. Surveys – survey research can be done online by providing a link to an automatic form that calculates the results, or you can produce it in a paper format. Surveys can give insight into how your customers feel about your price point, your brand, and the product or service they received.

With many of the different types of market research, businesses choose to offer something in return to their audience. Remember when I told you, your potential clients are always thinking about 'what's in it for me?' – this is no different. Businesses may offer a voucher, gift card, or coupon as an incentive. If you offer an incentive, your audience is more likely to participate in your survey.

Market research allows you to understand the viability of your business, and its products/services. It helps you to gain insight into the demand, and how your business may perform in reality. Not only is it important when you're first beginning, but it's also key for growth and success.

Research plays a huge part in finding out who your target audience is by testing what works. It helps to develop strong customer satisfaction and increases loyalty to your brand. It gives you much more information than you think. For example, if a product isn't selling, you may need to tweak it rather than alter your price point. Market research can help you identify exactly what you need to do.

When researching you need to ask yourself:

1. Is there a desire (by customers) for my product or service?
2. How many people would be interested in buying from me?
3. How would I rate the level of income and employment in my industry?
4. Where do my customers live and is there a limit to my reach?
5. What is the price point for similar products or services?

6. What similar products or services are already out there, and how can I make mine unique?

In the final section, it's time to identify the business that matches your skills...

How to Identify the Business that Matches Your Skills

In the previous chapter, I introduced you to a range of online business ideas, but it can be difficult to identify which business best matches your skills. There are strategies you can use to figure this out.

Let's consider your skills...

1. You've already considered the first step in the last chapter, so you should've narrowed down your ideas already – take your final few ideas and consider your:

- Knowledge
- Hobbies
- Education
- Passions

Think about how these things fit well with your business ideas. It's best to have a business idea that closely matches your skills and expertise, but you should also be passionate about it as this will keep you motivated.

2. Based on your final ideas, find a problem in the market that your product or service will solve. Consider the skills you have and consider how you can resolve this problem while also adding extra value for your clients.

3. Define your target market – based on your business idea/s, who will your products or services be aimed at? Where is the gap in the market and what gap will you fill? You may want to flip back to chapter 7 to refresh the ways of identifying your target audience as this will help you identify your target market by exploring the characteristics of your ideal client. Both your target market and target audience should link together as they must synchronize in order for your business to work.

Now you've explored your target market, it's time to move to the next step. This involves finding the right platform for freelancing. The platform you choose is also a key component for your success. You've made excellent progress so far. Let's keep going just a bit more.

10

FINDING THE RIGHT PLATFORM FOR FREELANCING

*W*hen I started out as a freelancer, it took me a while to figure out the right platform. That's why this chapter is all about freelancing and the best online platforms available if you want to begin your freelancing business right now.

While freelancing does require some planning, once you work out the logistics, there's no reason why you can't get started right away, even while you still work full-time. Let's jump in immediately by giving an overview of freelancing as a career and how beneficial it truly is.

Freelancing – What is it and Why is it Beneficial?

Freelancing is often seen as being a great way to earn some extra cash, but many people form a career and earn a full-time income from freelancing. You

122

aren't employed by one company, so you can work with several businesses/individuals at the same time and as a freelancer, you have the power to choose who you work with, when you do the work, and how you do it.

Some people view freelancing as daunting, but this is when I truly found freedom and flexibility. It's the point I truly became my own boss, and while it was a bit of a learning curve, it was truly a positive experience!

There are many benefits of freelancing, and they include:

1. Freedom and flexibility – as a parent, you don't have to worry about childcare when you're freelancing as you have full control over your working schedule. It fits around your family commitments and allows you to work on your own time, how long you work, and where you work. While you will obviously have to put in the hours, you are in control.

2. Being your own boss – working for yourself means you make all of the business decisions, and you choose what projects you work on, and what you don't. You are not confined by your boss. Being your own boss is liberating, and it means you can continue to grow as an entrepreneur. There may be some skills you need to learn, but many freelancers are happy to learn more so they can develop.

3. Money – when you're a freelancer, you may not see a huge increase in your salary at first, but once you grow your business and build your reputation, you can start to earn more and outsource the work to others, building your own small company. While you need to be competitive, you can grow your business and start to offer different products/services that take up less of your time, but allow you to increase your earnings. This includes semi-passive or passive income streams, which means you continue to earn money through an automated system and therefore don't need to do any (or much) extra work. Once you're an established expert, you can begin to serve more than one customer at once, which means your income will increase further.

4. There's no need to commute to work – if you're working online as a freelancer, you don't need to commute to work allowing you to save money. All you need is a laptop and a solid internet connection and you're in business. Many freelancers relocate to countries, leaving their expensive cities and moving to places where the cost of living is much cheaper. Becoming a nomad is a perk many love.

5. Build your skills – when I look back, I can't believe how much I've grown as an online

entrepreneur. I've improved so many soft skills along the way, and there are many things I've had to learn to do. Even though I was already a good communicator, I've had to learn to communicate online. Although I'm an expert in my niche, I've still grown my skills to the next level, which has allowed me to strengthen my claim as a leading expert. I know I'll never stop learning and growing, as freelancing is an ever-evolving business and there's always something new to learn.

What Kind of Jobs Opportunities Come With Freelancing?

Many people begin their freelancing career as a side hustle whilst they're still employed. This is a great way to test if freelancing works for you, and also allows you to try different jobs and projects to see which ones suit you best. Testing can help you decide what type of business will work best for you when you go solo.

Freelancing is for you if you're good at managing your time, are confident when putting in proposals or bids for new jobs or projects, and if you are self-disciplined and able to stick to deadlines. A good freelancer is also a good communicator, very professional, and works with both passion and initiative. *Does this sound like you?*

If it does, freelancing is perfect for you!

There are many job opportunities when it comes to

freelance work. While we talked through some online business ideas in the previous section, we did refer to freelancing as well. While some of the opportunities discussed below may have been mentioned briefly, not all have. There are many freelance opportunities available in the following sectors:

- Development and IT
- Design and Creative
- Sales and Marketing
- Admin and Support
- Writing and Translation
- Finance and Accounts
- Human Resource
- Engineering and Architecture
- Legal

Some of the highest-paying freelance opportunities exist in the following sectors:

- Digital Marketing
- Video Editing
- Web Development
- Graphic Design
- Content Writing

As you can see, there are many different freelancing opportunities out there. All you have to do is choose the right platform, so you can start earning.

The Best Freelancing Platforms

There are many freelancing platforms out there, so let's look at the top 5 and explore the pros and cons of each. This will help you decide which you believe will work best for you. I also recommend doing some research into each before you settle on one.

1. Toptal – an amazing option for top freelancers.

- Pros – Toptal is great as it offers high-end positions to freelancers, along with lucrative rewards. They screen you rigorously, so they ensure only the best freelancers are able to source positions that are often listed by large, successful companies, such as Microsoft.
- Cons – Toptal has a high barrier when it comes to the freelancers it admits to its portal. In fact, it's believed that only 3% of applicants are successfully listed.

2. Upwork – a popular platform, best for freelancer reviews and verifications.

- Pros – Upwork can lead to long-term contracts and is ideal for complex projects.
- Cons – while there are plenty of high-paid opportunities available, there are lots of low-quality workers, which can give freelancers a bad name.

3. Guru – one of the largest freelance marketplaces.

- Pros – Guru is a large marketplace so there is a huge customer base at your disposal. They also offer freelancer verification, so that your customers can see you are a legitimate client. Registration is also free.
- Cons – although it's free to join, Guru charges high fees on each job you complete, which is deducted from your earnings.

4. Freelancer.com – easy to use and offers a variety of payment methods.

- Pros – communication is easy on Freelancer, and there is a variety of freelancers available. The platform itself is competitive so there is a mix of high-quality or well-paid work, and low-paid or low-quality work.
- Cons – Freelancer is potentially expensive.

5. People Per Hour – Well known for certifying trustworthy freelancers.

- Pros – More than a million businesses use this site, which means there are many opportunities available and there is a massive international community. The platform is straightforward to use.

- Cons – while there are many positives of using People Per Hour, many people report that customer support is poor.

There are many platforms that can help freelancers look for opportunities, but in order to successfully earn money, you must win clients. Let's look at this now!

How to Win Your First Freelance Clients

Now you know where to go to find clients as a free-lancer, you still have to win your first project from a client. When you're brand new, it's a little more diffi-cult to show your credibility. The good news is, if you have set up your website and social media channels, you have somewhere to signpost your potential clients to show you're legitimate. Sometimes, a client will also ask for samples of your work, so bear that in mind.

There are 5 key steps you need to follow in order to win your first freelance client. They include:

1. Identify your skill and promote it as a service – we've mentioned the sectors earlier in this chapter, so let's say you have a background in office work, you could explore admin and support as a skill. You would then consider how working in this sector might look like, indicating what tasks you do well. Don't worry too much about this as you can tweak it later, but you should take a look at the

profiles of other successful freelancers in your field to see how they promote their skills.

2. Find your market or target audience – so again, let's use admin and support as our sector to give an example of how to find your target audience/market. Think about who would need this service. That could be small business owners or solopreneurs, who can't afford to employ permanent members of staff to cover their admin needs, or who need a job done urgently as they've lost a member. In that case, market to them.

3. Build your profile – when you're a freelancer, your profile is extremely important as you need to prove to your potential clients that you are trustworthy. A website is a great place to start. You can tell your own professional story, and add testimonials. Some platforms allow you to set up your personal profile there, so add some work samples, make sure your testimonials are clear, write blog posts to share your expertise, and have a clear presence on your social media channels. A good profile will show you take your work seriously and builds credibility. Professionalism is everything.

4. Market yourself to your target audience – when you're a freelancer, it's your job to

market yourself to your clients. Reach out to them using platforms (we've mentioned five in the previous section), and this includes social media platforms, such as LinkedIn.

5. Consider your results or gaps at each step in the process, and tweak your approach until you get it right – make sure you monitor your progress, so you can make any necessary tweaks to the application process. Think about:

- Why your proposal may have been rejected? You can even ask the client for feedback if you wish.
- How many people have you reached out to, based on the number of people who responded?
- Who are the people who are successful in your niche and what are they doing differently? Don't forget to research!
- Is there anything different in your niche or with how similar freelancers are conducting their business?

You need to analyze the data and look for gaps and areas for improvement in reference to each data point above. Tweak your process by restructuring, polishing, and rewriting your future proposals.

Once you get your first client and you have your proposal formula mastered, the work will start to flow, but it still takes your commitment and attention to apply for each project your take on. Make sure you always ask your clients to post a review for you. It makes a huge difference in attracting more work.

Freelancer Lisa - My Story

There is a belief that freelancers never earn enough money, but if you stop referring to freelancers, and begin referring to business owners, attitudes change. The freelancer is ultimately in charge of their own business, so sometimes, changing a simple word can change our perception.

Lisa is an Environmental Activist and Educator, who works as a freelancer, and her story has been a huge success, even though she is happy to call herself a freelancer, rather than a business owner.

When she was a child, Lisa traveled a lot and was talented in the sciences. Her father wanted her to pursue the sciences, but in her heart, Lisa's focus always belonged to environmental issues. Lisa has been able to take her love of the environment and transfer it to her freelancing success as a business consultant. As she works from home, Lisa offsets her carbon footprint every time she takes on a freelancing task – this includes planting trees and raising money for environmental charities. She helps businesses offset their carbon footprint and embrace more environmentally friendly policies and practices to reduce their carbon emissions. She continues to volunteer with environmental charities and also offers online sessions to educate people on environmental impacts. She has recently been asked to write an online course that focuses on greener businesses and has been asked to visit local schools. This is because she's built up her reputation and is well-known for her expertise in her local area.

We've talked about freelancing platforms and winning your first customer, but in chapter 11, I'll talk you through creating a customer base. Freelancers often get returning clients, so let's talk through how you can secure customer loyalty.

11

CREATING YOUR CUSTOMER BASE

*W*hen you're running your own business, it's important to find and retain your clients, so you can convert them into loyal, returning customers.

In this chapter, I am going to focus on helping you build your customer base, by giving you practical tips for building strong communication channels with potential customers, so that you can win them over and make money. We'll also talk about ways to build a true connection with your clients, ensuring their loyalty.

Creating a customer base doesn't have to be complicated, so by the end of this chapter, you'll know what you have to do!

How to Build a Loyal Customer Base

The secret to business longevity is building a strong

134

customer base. Customer loyalty stems from customer satisfaction, and if you have loyal customers, you will have repeat business, recommendations, higher conversion rates, and boosted profits.

It's certainly worth building because it can save you money in the long run. Searching for new customers costs you time (and money). Loyal customers recommend you to others so you don't have to spend a ton of time constantly searching. These are the steps to take to start building:

1. Get to know your customers – everyone loves a more personalized service, so if you get to know your customers and you allow them to get to know you, it's likely you'll gain their loyalty. Sharing information about yourself helps to build trust with your brand.

2. Reward your customers – developing rewards for your customers, such as a customer loyalty program is a great way to build a loyal customer base. There are many ways you can do this, from free gifts to discounts, to apps for those who make regular purchases.

3. Follow your values and utilize your strengths – you need to consider what's unique about your business, what you value the most, and what your business does best. All of these questions frame your brand, and if you have a solid brand, it's easier to attract loyal

customers. For example, if you want to show your clients you're reliable, you can show it by being consistent with your marketing and staying loyal to your customers. It's a give-and-take.

4. Set up a referral system – this is a little like the loyalty program we talked about in point 2. This means that if your customer refers other customers to the business, they get a reward for doing it. Incentivizing referrals is really effective as it keeps your current customers loyal, while also bringing in new ones.

5. Encourage your customers to give you feedback – trust is a two-way relationship and if you really want to show your customers how much you trust and value them, encourage them to give you feedback. Showing that you're always willing to improve encourages more business with your customers, and they'll be happy to do further business because they'll see that you value their insights.

6. Engage with customers on social media channels – customer relationships are often improved by social media presence. There's an expectation amongst certain clients, that most businesses are visible online, so being active and present is key to nurturing your customers. This is a great way to stay on their

radar and if you build a strong online community, it encourages them to come back with more business, more frequently.

7. Store your customers' data – your customer will want things to be easy for them, so to make it easier, store their customer data (with their permission), so next time they make a purchase, their information is already there. Buying doesn't have to be complicated, so make your store as easy to use as possible and offer great customer support as this will also strengthen customer relations.

These steps show that building customer loyalty begins with connection and personalization. It's imperative that your message is tailored to your target audience, and one way to do this is to personalize it to your customers. Taking on board their feedback allows you to improve customer satisfaction further and take it to the next level.

How to Build Strong Communication Channels with Potential Customers

It's important for you to build strong communication with your potential customers, as this helps you build a strong connection. There's nothing better than when you're made to feel special by your client, *right?*

If you build strong communication, it means your clients will find you more approachable. This is important to me because if my clients have an idea or a problem that I can resolve, I want to know about it. Again, it's about the all-important 'T' word – TRUST, because strong communication is built on a foundation of both trust and respect.

To build strong communications with your clients, there are 4 things you need to do:

1. Build an emotional connection with the client – this ensures your client feels able to come to you if they have a problem. Try to understand their situation and remedy any conflict easily. There are 4 key components to increasing your emotional connection, and this includes:

- Self-awareness – this means understanding how you respond to certain emotions.
- Social awareness – this means having an understanding of professional etiquette, your obligations as their supplier, and being aware of the social setup.
- Self-management – this means you're aligned with your thoughts and can control emotions so that they don't become overpowering.
- Empathy – this means you are able to understand your client's perspective. It's putting yourself in their shoes, so you can comprehend and respond appropriately.

If you get these things right, you'll find that you have a strong emotional connection with your clients.

2. Ensure communication is clear and within context – sometimes, it's difficult to intuit communication, especially if there isn't clarity. Effective communication is expressed as simply as possible, so choose your words carefully, explain your perspective, and ensure you are respectful of the person who is receiving your communication. This helps to avoid confusion, so if you're honest and clear when it comes to communication, it's less likely that your client will misinterpret what you're saying. Keep it concise – less is best!

3. It's not what you say, it's the way you say it – your tone can get you because tone can't always be intuited. Tone and voice are key to how others perceive what you're saying. Your voice should consistently be you, don't try to be someone you're not. When you use the right tone, it shows respect, and it can make difficult conversations easier to digest and remedy. With this in mind, when you're communicating with your clients:

- Remain friendly, ensuring you are courteous and sincere.
- Use a neutral tone unless you're purposely expressing emotion.
- Use simple language that does not show bias or discrimination.

- Let your confidence flow – show you believe in what you say.
- Always keep in mind this question – 'How does this benefit my client?'

4. Listen actively to your clients – you don't want them to feel undervalued. You can do this by focusing on them, summarizing what they've said to you, and using body language and acknowledgments such as nodding your head or saying 'yes' at intervals in between the conversation. Make sure you remain engaged and ask questions, as active listening can prevent delays, help to avoid confusion, and create a more productive relationship without wasting time.

Now, you've strengthened communication with your clients. It's time to think about winning more clients...

How to Win More Clients

When you're in business, it's important to win clients, but not just any clients, I want you to win the best clients. *But how can you ensure that happens?*

Every time you land a client, you've put energy and resources into it, so when you're trying to win clients, your efforts should be rewarded by winning the best clients for your business.

The best clients are ultimately YOUR kind of people – they're the people who are meant to buy your products/services. They're the people who need you to solve their problems, and they are the people who have strong connections with – they soon know, like, and trust you, so they are loyal, and they are the people you want to be dealing with day in, day out.

There are 5 things you can do to ensure you're getting the best clients, consistently:

1. Know who your clients are – if you want the best clients for your business, you need to know who they are. We've done some work figuring this out already, so well done, this step is done.

2. Network online or in person – it's really important to be seen, so you can connect with your potential clients. One way to do this is to network online or in person. You can attend other people's groups on Facebook and give sound advice, you can use live videos on your social media so your audience can ask you questions, or you can offer to do talks in places where your target audience hangs out. The main thing is, to hang around in the same places as your target audience, show up and give value, and engage with them to build a solid connection.

3. Do something helpful for the community – if you're passionate about a specific charity or your local community, it's good to help out if you're in the position to. Everyone loves a

good news story, and when you're passionate about something, it gives you common ground with your target audience and it also tells them about your character and values. There are many people who attempt to offset their carbon footprint or give back to environmental or animal charities. They may also raise money for cancer charities, give food to the food bank, or set up a fundraiser on their website to raise money for children's charities. Heading to a soup kitchen to head up, painting the church fence, or cleaning up a park in your area shows you care about the community.

4. Collaborate with other companies – teaming up with others is an amazing thing to do. There are many benefits because you learn from the other person or business, whilst also gaining exposure to their client base. This increases your presence, demonstrates credibility, and shows that you're a team player. If you build up positive relationships with other businesses, they could refer relevant clients to you, and you can return the favor. It's a win-win.

5. Make your clients feel special – if you get to know your clients, you can make them feel special. This helps you win them over, and remember, everyone, is special. You can make people feel good by remembering their

names and asking them questions about their life, their family, or how they feel. Doing this creates a positive bond, so make a conscious effort to add a personal touch when it comes to your clients, and make them feel special.

In this chapter, I've provided you with many tips to help you grow your customer base in a positive way, and we've talked about the importance of loyal customers. You've explored the strategies to building a customer base, whilst also developing strong communication strategies. Connection with your clients is undeniably important, and truly connecting with your customers ends the hustle of having to find more clients over and over again. You've also explored 5 things you can do to win more ideal clients, and all these things are vital components when creating your customer base.

For the last point here, I just want to mention the importance of connection one more time as we've touched on this in all three sections of his chapter. Personalizing your approach to your customers, without trying too hard is a key way to build connection. The reason I'm stressing that you shouldn't try too hard is that we've talked about the know, like, and trust factor quite a lot, but trying too hard comes across as desperate. Whilst you should work to build connections, you still need to be yourself, because your clients value honesty and respect!

"Communication - the human connection - is the key to personal and career success."
~ *Paul J. Meyer*

As we move on to the final chapter, we're going to talk about the ways you can scale your business using automation. This is my favorite part, so don't go anywhere – the best is yet to come!

SECTION IV

Developing Passive Income Streams

12

SCALING UP YOUR BUSINESS THROUGH AUTOMATION

*N*ow you're ready to start your business, and you're working on growing your customer base, it's important to consider your next steps. You see, in business, you always have to stay a step ahead of the game, which is why this final chapter is the ideal place to start discussing how you can scale up your business.

To truly succeed in business, you need to plan for the future. Ask yourself, *what do you want your business to look like in 12 months? Or 5 years? And even 10 years?*

I want you to succeed in your business, and I know you want to as well, so it's important to spend some time focusing on the long term. In this chapter, you'll focus on the impact of technology in business, as well as discuss some strategies to help you kick-start automation. We'll finish off by exploring the different systems and processes in your business that can be automated.

It's time to leverage the power of automation!

Technology and Business – Understanding the Impact

The use of technology in business has been growing over several years, but its growth rate increased when the pandemic hit in 2020, and it has been growing ever since. This increased as more and more people are online than ever before, so it's the perfect place to grow your business because it opens up doors to customers that a few years ago wouldn't have been possible.

Technology has impacted traditional ways of growing your business because we no longer need to meet in person – we can meet with people across the other side of the world, by clicking just one button. Social media allows us to network with businesses and people from all different industries, careers, backgrounds, ages, genders, and beliefs, and having access to such a network has opened up new opportunities and provided us with more connections than ever before.

The impact of technology doesn't stop there. Technology can also be used to do a job for us. If we want posts to live on social media, we can use scheduling tools to make this happen. We can set up email sequences using specific software, so when people sign up for our websites, they receive a series of ordered emails that allow you to keep in touch with your clients. There's no doubt, it makes things easier for both you and your client, as it's productive, offers a better quality of service, and is much more efficient.

Technology has changed the way we operate our business. The power of the internet has allowed us to work remotely, from anywhere, whilst still being able to access the files which we have stored in the cloud. This means we can access our files from anywhere, by simply logging in.

Technology has also changed the way we record, monitor, and analyze our analytics and capture data. AI and ML systems use models that automatically do this for us, provide accurate forecasts, and highlight when something performs well. This means we simply have to look to see what's working and tweak it. Customer service has also improved, as certain messaging systems can communicate with automated responses to customer requests. Of course, this doesn't answer every question but can work for some which mean there are fewer customer service queries to respond to. This frees up your time.

Technology allows us to learn online as well, as more and more training and education are becoming available online.

Automation is great. If you use it to your advantage, you will work less on the details and can focus more on service delivery.

Technology helps businesses, especially small businesses that can't necessarily afford to employ staff members to speed up their systems and take the pressure off. This enhances their business, improves their income, and helps to increase productivity. This means the business is more secure and could look to employ staff in the future, as it is able to scale at a faster pace.

There's no doubt that technology is changing the way we do business, but we must embrace it and leverage the opportunity it brings, to allow us to grow and scale. When you have less staff, there's less of a chance a human error might occur, because technology makes fewer mistakes and can complete many of the repetitive, manual tasks that no one likes to do. This increases efficiency as well as quality.

Strategies to Automate Your Business

There are many ways you can automate your business. It's used widely as part of business processes because it helps you scale at a more rapid rate. If you want to scale your business with automation, there are five strategies you can follow to help automate your business:

1. List the things you want to automate – to find out what you want to automate, write a list of all the repetitive tasks that take up your time, and while they're essential, they offer very little value. This could be anything from sending out emails, following up on direct messages, sending out responses, answering

questions, building your email list, sending responses, or scheduling your social media posts.

2. Find the right automation systems for you – once you decide to automate your business, it's best to do some research and find a few good tools, that can automate as many of these time-consuming tasks as possible. This makes your business run much more smoothly. If you're aware of the procedures you follow already or have a standard operating procedure (SOP) in place already, you can figure out if automation can take place. Your automated systems require you to have clear steps in place. This way, mistakes are less likely!

3. Figure out what your priorities are – if you've identified many areas for automation, be sure to prioritize your list so you can automate the process that will be most beneficial to you, first. Try to focus on processes that take you a lot of time and occur regularly, as this will free up more of your time to work on the things that matter. When prioritizing, always consider how it will improve your process and if it will have a positive impact on your customers.

4. I can't afford to automate my systems yet, what should I do? – there are some amazing

systems out there that cost money, but it's best to start off simple and start off with those that are free, or free at least until your business grows. There are many free systems and project management software that can help you meet your automation goals, while you get yourself established.

5. Plan for future automation – there are parts of the business that cannot be automated, so for the time being, concentrate on those that can and think about the future. Your business goals will stir you in the direction you need to go. If you grow quicker than anticipated as a result of your automation, you could reach your goals at a quicker rate, so make sure you have a plan for the future and recognize how automation can help you scale your business and accelerate growth in the long term.

The question that's left here is what you should automate, and in the final section, we're going to talk through this in detail.

What to Automate?

There are many processes and systems that you can automate within your business. Automation can ultimately help you take your business to the next level and can certainly help to boost your sales. When you're starting out in business, it's important to make the best use of your time, and automation is the key to freeing this up.

There are many different things you can automate, including:

- Invoicing and billing – it's important to manage your finances well, and it's important that you invoice and bill your clients effectively. There are apps and systems out there that will automate this for you, such as Stripe, Paypal, and Wise. If you build their payment button into your sales page or store, they can help you retrieve payments and will send invoices on your behalf automatically. You can also use these systems to request payments manually.
- Data backup – this is crucial for a successful, trustworthy business as it ensures data, including that of your customers is backed up and kept safe. It's not always easy to remember to do this, so automating it helps you maintain a positive reputation with your clients and saves you time. A popular data backup app is Cloud Backup. It's easy to use and is a popular automated process.
- Accounting and expense tracking – there are many systems out there that allow you to manage your accounting and expense

tracking. Some bank accounts offer add-on apps that take care of your accounting and expense tracking. Accounting software can even pay your bills for you on the relevant dates, and process invoices received. You can also use batch processing systems to automate your transactions. Batch processing can raise invoices, and statements, and also run payroll reports.

- Sales and CRM – sales and CRM systems can help you search for leads, invoice your clients, process your orders, track any mailed items, and help to manage your customer base. Email systems are examples of CRMs as they improve communication with your clients overall. While an algorithm can never negotiate a deal and provide that personalized touch for your client, it can complete the tasks above quickly, which can free up some of your time.

- Customer support – customer service and support can also be automated. You can send emails through a CRM system, such as Active Campaign, MailerLite, or MailChimp. There are also apps that send text messages, and then there are chatbot tools as well, that send messages to you in Facebook messenger. All of these can keep you in touch with your customers and offer support while you focus on something on building your business. With chatbot systems, people can often type in questions, and you can program it to respond with the most likely answer or many answers for that matter.

- Communication – we've mentioned communication with customers in customer support, sales, and CRM, but communication takes place in a variety of ways. You can program your emails to send an automatic response, and if you still send letters, there is a mailing system on word processing packages that prints the same letter to the people on your mailing list if you want to send them a letter. Communication automation often helps you stay organized. If you need to communicate through social media, this too can be automated through systems like Hootsuite, or through the social media channel directly. This means that social media posts will be posted at times of your choice throughout the day and you don't have to do this manually. If your customers call you, having a personalized greeting on your voicemail can also improve customer relations, and there's an automated system for collecting your messages. Automation can also help set up repeat meetings, events, and reminders in your calendar system and on video

conferencing systems such as Zoom or
Microsoft Teams.

Technology can certainly be leveraged to help you
run and scale your business. Business automation is
certainly beneficial, as it provides you with clarity
when it comes to all your processes, which allows your
business to function efficiently.

It also allows you to standardize your operations,
which eliminates human error in your daily tasks.
Human error can cost you time and money. Your work-
flows also become streamlined due to automation in
business. Business processes are easy to follow, but as
they are clear, you gain greater accountability, and can
easily monitor how the processes are performing.
Productivity increases in both instances here, because
wasteful activities are minimized.

What will you do with all of your free time?

At the start of this chapter, we mentioned passive
income, so before we end this chapter, it's important to
recognize how you can use automation to create
streams of passive income. Let's say you produce an
online, self-led course…

You are selling this course, so first, you'll market it
by advertising, but this is where automation kicks in.
You'll have a button that leads to a landing page that
provides the details of the course you're selling, and the
customer reads through it and makes a decision
whether to buy or not. If they click to leave, a pop-up
appears and asks them if they're sure they want to leave

without buying. If they say yes, that's the end of the process. If they decide to buy, they click to buy and are taken to a sales page in which they are invited to pay, and with one click, they are taken to Stripe to add their card details. Stripe then bills them, and sends them an invoice confirming the sale, but in the meantime, the person has been sent to another page that says 'Thank you for your purchase, please check your email' and it's at this point, that your email CRM system sends them course log-in details and a link to the course website – again, all automated as the course website can be linked to payments and to your email management system.

If you produce an ebook on Amazon the process is even simpler, as the book is advertised or found on Amazon and your client buys your book, Amazon records the purchase and deposits your royalties directly in your bank account monthly. You can also publish your book on Audible, so now you have doubled your income streams.

Automation means you basically earn money while you sleep!

The automation is set up in advance, so your products can be bought over and over. The orders are processed for you and when you wake the next day, you'll have emails confirming that people have bought your items. This is your passive income stream, and you can set up as many streams as you like.

Now that you have a taste, I want you to know that this is just the beginning, automation and passive income can be so much more.

Keep dreaming, keep scaling, and keep striving for success!

And remember...

"Business opportunities are like buses, there's always another one coming."
~ Richard Branson

So keep your eyes open...

AFTERWORD

You've made it! You've learned online business secrets for women beginners, and you're ready to kickstart your own online business. You've crushed your limiting beliefs by bashing your excuses and squashing the lies about starting your own business.

Becoming a business owner is a journey, but you've mentally prepared yourself for take-off by finding your 'why' and exploring the reasons why entrepreneurship is for you—knowing your 'why' has increased your motivation, which has driven you to overcome the fears and doubts you have about starting your own business. We've focused on how your brain processes information and reacts; we've looked at your memory and physical health and contemplated how fear affects you and your mental health.

Together, we've faced the fears, and we've also had the talk...

You know, the talk that makes people uncomfortable. The money talk. We've talked about preparing financially for entrepreneurship, and we've even reflected on how and when is the right time to quit your day job.

Along your journey, you've:

- Improved your time management skills
- Considered all the skills you have, and
- Took them into account as you defined your niche

You've also worked to assess your options by choosing the right online business for you, reviewed your freelancing opportunities, and looked to the future by exploring ways to build your customer base and scale your business by embracing passive income streams and automation strategies.

You have all the tools you need to start your online business, and now is the time to embrace your power. You're officially an entrepreneur – say it aloud! I'm an entrepreneur. You have to believe it first, then make it happen.

No longer do you:

1. Lack of direction when it comes to your career.

2. Crave flexibility – you know it's within your grasp.
3. Worry about your poor work-life balance.
4. Fear missing out on life's enjoyment and spending time with your family.
5. Stress that your income is limited because you know it's up to you to find more ways to bring in the money, and you're well-prepared to reel it in.

You have the necessary skills to earn money online and have the power to work on your own terms. Like me, I want you to build your 6-figure empire and get the flexibility you desire, but it's up to you to take action.

You have proved your worth through and through, so you have the confidence to act on your desire. You can have exactly what you want as it's in the palm of your hand, and I know how amazing you are. Believe me, I have coached thousands of women like you, and I know you have what it takes. Just believe it and take the first step.

Now you have all the information you need to start your own online business, put it to good use, and work towards your dreams.

Becoming an online entrepreneur is a distant dream, no more. All you need to do is practice the strategies and use the tools shared in this book to achieve your goals.

It's time to make the transition so you can ditch the 9-5 and embrace the career you desire and deserve.

FROM THE AUTHOR

By now I hope you are getting excited about all the possibilities that exist for you to make some really good money online. If you are starting out while you still hold a full-time job, that's awesome! Six months from now, you will have a well-established online business, and you can fire your boss, as they say.

 If this book helped you take the first steps towards financial freedom, I invite you to take 5 minutes of your time and leave me your honest feedback on Amazon. You may not know that for self-publishers, feedback is really important. It helps us spread the word about our books, and it helps those who are

looking for this type of information find it when they need it most. I invite you to take 2 minutes *right now, scan the QR code below* or hover over it and leave me your honest feedback. I am really, really grateful.

YOUR FREE GIFT

I want to offer you a gift to say thank you for purchasing this book. It's my bestselling ebook, "Leadership For The New Female Manager." Whether you currently have a job or are just starting out on your own, your leadership skills are responsible for your success at work or in business. *Scan or hover over the QR code below* or email me at karina@karinag sanchez.com, and I will send you a digital copy of my book!

SPECIAL BONUS!

Want this book for FREE?

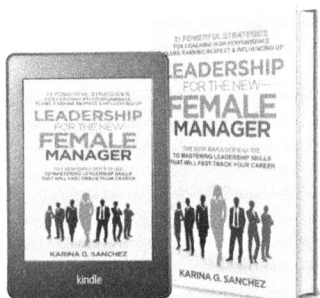

Get FREE unlimited access to it and all of my books by joining our community!

Scan with your camera to join!

In the *Leadership For The New Female Manager* book, you'll discover:

- How to overcome imposter syndrome and feel comfortable leading people, even if you don't have as much experience as everyone else.
- How to evaluate your natural strengths, talents, and attributes, then use them to boost your influence in the workplace.

- A deep understanding of the human side of leadership that you won't find anywhere else to help you grow your leadership skills.
- How to draw information out of people in a gentle, authentic way and use the feedback to progress within your organization.

...... and much more

JOIN OUR PRIVATE FACEBOOK GROUP

If you haven't already joined our amazing **Private Facebook Group of Women** who are either starting their own businesses or are already entrepreneurs, I invite you to join us. Scan or hover over the QR code below.

ABOUT THE AUTHOR

Karina G. Sanchez is a certified Business Coach helping female entrepreneurs reach their full potential. She has inspired hundreds of leaders and entrepreneurs to reach for the stars and achieve personal and professional success. *This is* her true passion! She has helped countless female leaders overcome imposter syndrome, which kept them from achieving incredible results for themselves, their teams, and their lives.

She has lived and worked internationally and has

consulted in the retail, pharmaceutical, and financial industries, to name a few. Her energy and passion have brought a positive change within small and large teams alike. She has an uncanny ability to open minds to new and innovative ways of thinking, helping individuals reach their financial potential.

She has written two bestselling books that have generated 6-figure incomes for many female entrepreneurs working from the comfort of their own homes. Her mission is to fill every woman's life with joy and financial abundance.

---

facebook.com/Karina-G-Sanchez-Consulting-112840551328381

instagram.com/karina.g.sanchez

linkedin.com/in/karina-g-sanchez-0b446216

tiktok.com/@karinag.sanchez

youtube.com/@karinagsanchez

amazon.com/author/karina.g.sanchez

PARTING QUOTE

"All your dreams can come true if you have the courage to pursue them."

~ Walt Disney

BIBLIOGRAPHY

https://www.alphagamma.eu/entrepreneurship/99-quotes-about-entrepreneurship/#:~:text=99%20inspiring%20quotes%20about%20entrepreneurship%201%201.%20%E2%80%9CSuccess,coaster%20ride%20than%20a%20cruise.%E2%80%9D%20...%20More%20items

https://www.medicalnewstoday.com/articles/321018#21-signs

https://www.hyperhidrosiscumc.com/signs-of-nervousness-nervousness-body-language/

https://brandft.co.uk/stress-and-exams/?msclkid=3ab1cb817b721e0b8a54a8cf6a8b7d0b&utm_source=bing&utm_medium=cpc&utm_campaign=Brand%20Financial%20Training%20Ltd%20DSA&utm_term=brandft%20co&utm_content=All%20Webpages

https://www.waterford.org/education/kids-who-changed-the-world/

https://www.boostoxygen.com/4-real-life-examples-age-just-number/

https://www.abundancenolimits.com/business-affirmations/#:~:text=Daily%20affirmations%20for%20entrepreneurs%201%201%201%20choose%20to,ready%20for%20another%20great%20productive%20day.%20More%20items

https://growthlab.com/10-ways-to-start-a-business-when-you-dont-have-enough-time/

https://www.inc.com/melanie-curtin/attention-millennials-average-entrepreneur-is-this-old-when-they-found-their-first-startup.html#:~:text=The%20facts%20clearly%20suggest%20one%20side%20over%20the,leaders%20of%20high-growth%20startups%20is%2045%20years%20old.

https://www.inc.com/yuriy-boykiv/starting-a-business-in-your-40s-makes-more-sense-than-you-think.html

https://www.interaction-design.org/literature/article/15-popular-reasons-to-become-a-freelancer-or-entrepreneur

https://www.creativeboom.com/tips/20-great-reasons-to-go-freelance/

https://www.upwork.com/resources/advantages-of-being-a-freelancer

https://lifehacks.io/10-reasons-why-freelancing-is-better-than-any-job/

https://www.forbes.com/sites/kathycaprino/2016/02/08/ready-to-leave-your-corporate-job-and-start-freelancing-heres-what-you-need-to-know/?sh=2ec85f746165

https://www.profitablefreelancer.com/why-millions-of-people-are-quitting-their-9-5-jobs-to-freelance

https://www.indiatoday.in/education-today/jobs-and-careers/story/5-reasons-you-should-think-of-shifting-to-freelance-jobs-1676648-2020-05-11

https://thetotalentrepreneurs.com/internet-entrepreneur/

https://www.entrepreneur.com/starting-a-business/4-reasons-why-an-online-business-is-the-best-investment-you/241759

https://www.mondaq.com/canada/advertising-marketing-branding/741090/5-ways-the-internet-has-changed-business

https://unctad.org/meeting/webinar-entrepreneurship-post-covid-19-resurgence-entrepreneurship-and-fintech

https://www.fastcompany.com/1824235/8-reasons-choose-startup-over-corporate-job

https://www.keyholemarketing.us/how-to-find-the-why-of-your-business-story/

https://www.tonyrobbins.com/stories/unleash-the-power/overcoming-fear-in-5-steps/

https://tinybuddha.com/blog/5-steps-to-overcome-fear-and-meet-your-goals/

https://medium.com/carl-pullein/why-your-fears-destroy-your-goals-77ebfcb2b0cd

https://www.forbes.com/sites/forbescoachescouncil/2018/03/29/overcoming-fear-and-achieving-your-goals-starts-with-one-simple-step/?sh=1da49633303d

https://www.healthline.com/health/anxiety/fear-of-success#strategies

https://www.lifehack.org/articles/communication/what-you-have-fear-success.html

https://www.forbes.com/sites/carolinecastrillon/2021/08/22/top-10-reasons-you-have-a-fear-of-success/?sh=385759be1c15

https://medium.com/swlh/why-your-afraid-of-success-3419e612f5e9

https://www.healthline.com/health/anxiety/fear-of-success

https://www.betterup.com/blog/fear-of-success

https://www.lifehack.org/articles/communication/what-you-have-fear-success.html

https://www.nm.org/healthbeat/healthy-tips/emotional-health/5-things-you-never-knew-about-fear

https://www.smithsonianmag.com/science-nature/what-happens-brain-feel-fear-180966992/

https://www.verywellmind.com/the-psychology-of-fear-2671696

https://www.takingcharge.csh.umn.edu/impact-fear-and-anxiety

https://www.goodreads.com/quotes/tag/overcoming-fear?page=2

https://www.wow4u.com/purpose-photo/

https://www.forbes.com/sites/robertberger/2014/04/30/top-100-money-quotes-of-all-time/?sh=6a0b0b2c4998

https://bettermoneyhabits.bankofamerica.com/en/saving-budgeting/creating-a-budget

https://edition.cnn.com/2021/11/24/success/financial-impact-quit-job-feseries/index.html

https://www.realsimple.com/work-life/life-strategies/job-career/money-steps-to-prepare-to-quit-your-job

https://hbr.org/2022/02/6-signs-its-time-to-leave-your-job

https://www.businessnewsdaily.com/6116-how-to-quit-your-job-without-burning-bridges.html

https://www.forbes.com/sites/carolinecastrillon/2021/07/21/what-to-do-before-quitting-your-job/?sh=38ecc1051396

https://www.forbes.com/advisor/personal-finance/prepare-finances-great-resignation/

https://www.businessinsider.com/personal-finance/how-much-money-do-i-need-to-quit-my-job?IR=T

https://www.fool.com/the-ascent/personal-finance/articles/6-ways-to-financially-prepare-for-quitting-your-job/

https://www.cnbc.com/select/how-to-create-a-budget-guide/

https://www.nerdwallet.com/article/finance/how-to-budget

https://www.investopedia.com/articles/pf/08/small-business-budget.asp

https://www.indeed.com/career-advice/career-development/activities-for-time-management-in-the-workplace

https://everhour.com/blog/top-time-management-games/

https://www.betterhelp.com/advice/time-management/types-and-examples-of-time-management-activities/

https://www.entrepreneur.com/living/3-steps-to-get-more-done-in-less-time/282295

https://hbr.org/2019/01/5-strategies-for-getting-more-work-done-in-less-time

https://unctad.org/meeting/webinar-entrepreneurship-post-covid-19-resurgence-entrepreneurship-and-fintech

https://www.bloomberg.com/opinion/articles/2021-06-01/how-covid-inspired-a-new-generation-of-entrepreneurs#xj4y7vzkg?leadSource=uverify%20wall

https://wyss.harvard.edu/news/entrepreneurship-in-the-era-of-covid-19/

https://blogs.worldbank.org/developmenttalk/how-did-covid-19-pandemic-influence-pace-new-business-formation

https://weidelonwinning.com/blog/build-your-confidence-by-identifying-your-strengths/

https://positivepsychology.com/self-worth/

https://www.goodhousekeeping.com/life/g38333580/self-love-quotes/#:~:text=%E2%80%9CBe%20yourself%2C%20but%20always%20your%20better%20self.%E2%80%9D&text=%E2%80%9CDon't%20sacrifice%20yourself%20too,nobody%20will%20care%20for%20you.%E2%80%9D&text=%E2%80%9CKeep%20taking%20time%20for%20yourself,you're%20you%20again.%E2%80%9D

https://hr.virginia.edu/sites/default/files/PDFs/Conducting_a_Self_Evaluation.pdf

https://wethrive.net/performance-reviews-and-appraisals/self-evaluation-important-for-development/

https://www.cio.com/article/289180/careers-staffing-10-tips-for-making-self-evaluations-meaningful.html

https://www.betterup.com/blog/the-importance-of-knowing-yourself

https://www.lifehack.org/articles/productivity/10-ways-identify-your-talents-and-utilize-them.html

https://www.verywellmind.com/why-it-s-important-to-have-high-self-esteem-5094127

https://www.robertwalters.co.uk/career-advice/keeping-your-career-on-track/skills-101-evaluate-your-skill-set.html

https://www.careeraddict.com/assessing-skills-career

https://www.monster.com/career-advice/article/assessing-your-skills

https://www.betterup.com/blog/full-potential

https://hbr.org/2008/07/reaching-your-potential

https://inspiringtips.com/asia/ways-to-unlock-your-full-potential/

https://www.lifehack.org/articles/communication/9-ways-reach-
your-fullest-potential-every-day.html

https://www.experian.co.uk/blogs/latest-thinking/small-business/6-
benefits-to-an-online-presence/#:~:text=If%20you%20have%20a%
20good,media%20platforms%20are%20both%20key

https://datareportal.com/global-digital-overview

https://www.marketingevolution.com/marketing-essentials/target-
audience#:~:text=Your%20target%20audience%20refers%20to,a%
20myriad%20of%20other%20factors

https://www.businessnewsdaily.com/6748-business-niche-
characteristics.html

https://www.betterup.com/blog/how-to-find-your-niche

https://blog.hubspot.com/sales/niche-market

https://www.entrepreneur.com/leadership/5-steps-you-can-use-to-
find-your-niche/272808

https://www.forbes.com/sites/johnrampton/2017/11/07/a-5-step-
formula-to-find-your-niche/?sh=2e1c87948fc0

https://www.thisweknow.org/the-significance-of-getting-your-busi
ness-online/

https://medium.com/@nyxonedigital/importance-of-e-commerce-
and-online-shopping-and-why-to-sell-online-5a3fd8e6f416

https://www.thebalancemoney.com/putting-offline-business-online-
2531853

https://www.hashmicro.com/blog/the-importance-of-online-market
ing-for-business/

https://www.legalzoom.com/articles/how-to-start-an-online-busi
ness-in-8-steps

https://www.entrepreneur.com/starting-a-business/how-to-start-a-
business-online/175242

https://www.godigit.com/become-an-agent/how-to-make-money-
online

https://www.forbes.com/sites/laurabegleybloom/2020/03/25/make-money-online-right-now/?sh=2d419e1870a5

https://www.nerdwallet.com/article/small-business/online-business-ideas

https://www.classycareergirl.com/how-to-narrow-down-business-idea-5-minutes/

https://www.investopedia.com/articles/forex/11/why-trade-forex.asp

https://www.freelanceuk.com/become/pros-and-cons-freelancing.shtml#:~:text=Freelancing%2C%20depending%20on%20your%20industry,still%20being%20able%20to%20work.

https://blog.marketresearch.com/4-business-goals-market-research-can-help-you-accomplish

https://blog.hubspot.com/marketing/market-research-buyers-journey-guide

https://www.investopedia.com/terms/m/market-research.asp

https://www.sba.gov/business-guide/plan-your-business/market-research-competitive-analysis

https://www.entrepreneur.com/starting-a-business/conducting-market-research/217388

https://www.entrepreneurshipinabox.com/190/how-to-find-a-business-ideas-that-match-your-own-skills/

https://www.businessnewsdaily.com/15751-conduct-market-analysis.html

https://www.upwork.com/resources/what-is-freelancing

https://razorpay.com/learn/what-are-freelance-jobs-a-guide-to-freelancing/

https://www.techradar.com/best/best-freelance-websites

https://www.freecodecamp.org/news/how-to-get-your-first-freelancing-client-project/

https://www.peppercontent.io/blog/freelance-success-stories/

https://blog.hubspot.com/marketing/10-ways-to-speak-to-customers-who-dont-know-they-need-you

https://hbr.org/2010/07/stop-trying-to-delight-your-customers

https://www.cloudways.com/blog/how-to-get-more-clients/

https://www.proofhub.com/articles/client-communication-skills

https://www.macquarie.com.au/advisers/improve-client-communication.html

https://www.zendesk.com/in/blog/build-customer-loyalty/

https://www.techtarget.com/searchcustomerexperience/feature/6-ways-to-build-customer-loyalty-for-your-business

https://www.businessnewsdaily.com/16017-build-customer-loyalty.html

https://www.brainyquote.com/topics/connection-quotes

https://www.projectmanager.com/blog/30-best-business-quotes

https://www.salesforce.com/blog/what-is-crm-your-business-nerve-center-blog/

https://www.forbes.com/sites/forbes-personal-shopper/2022/11/28/cyber-monday-engagement-ring-deals/?sh=12a914ef7712

https://www.forbes.com/sites/forbesdigitalcovers/2018/07/30/the-backsies-billionaire-texan-builds-second-fortune-from-wreckage-of-real-estate-empire-hed-sold/?sh=22c10d563a72

https://accelerationeconomy.com/automation/5-tips-to-scale-up-your-business-using-automation/

https://contractbook.com/blog/5-ways-to-scale-your-business-using-automation

https://www.zenbusiness.com/blog/7-business-tasks-that-can-be-automated-to-boost-revenue/

https://www.netsuite.com/portal/resource/articles/business-strategy/business-automation-examples.shtml

https://www.businessnewsdaily.com/9835-automation-tech-workforce.html

https://roboticsandautomationnews.com/2021/09/18/9-apps-to-auto mate-your-company-processes/46322/

https://www.ventureharbour.com/10-small-business-automation-tools-to-save-time-increase-profit/

https://www.getcloudapp.com/blog/marketing/business-process-automation/

https://www.inc.com/jeff-haden/300-motivational-quotes-to-inspire-you-to-achieve-your-dreams.html

Published by Virago Publishing
www.CorporateToFreelancer.com

THIS

Journal

BELONGS TO:

_____

Introduction

Starting an online business from home can be a great way for busy women to achieve financial independence and flexibility in their work schedules. With the rise of the internet and e-commerce, starting and running a successful business from the comfort of your own home is easier than ever. As a busy woman juggling work, family, and other responsibilities, starting an online business can be a perfect way to build a career that fits around your lifestyle. This allows you to work at your own pace, set your own hours, and control your own income. However, starting a successful online business does require careful planning, preparation, and execution.

Once you embark on this journey, it's essential to be patient, determined, and ready to learn new skills. This journal will help you set weekly goals, get into the habit of daily reflections on what went well and what could have been done better, will motivate you with weekly inspirations, and encourage you to put your thoughts on paper so that when you look back one year from now, you will see how far you have come.

I encourage you to record your experience, thoughts, feeling, and goals. Always strive to better yourself one day at a time because...

"As long as you don't give up, you can't lose."

When I set out to do this 1.5 years ago, I had no idea what type of impact a simple journal would have on my life. It was life-changing, and I want to do the same for you. So, follow me on this journey, and let's do this together.

Karina G. Sanchez

Begin the Process

How do we define unfounded excuses?
We tell ourselves lies that stop us in our tracks.

Take a few moments to think about what YOUR unfounded excuses are and write them below.

You can do this!

It's time to get motivated.
"Show Me How Good It Can Get"

List some of your own motivational phrases below:

How to create your 'Why'?
List all the reasons why this is important to you. NO judgment; just braindump it all on paper. Once you have an idea, form your "Why Mission Statement."

The reason why I want to have an Online Business is:

_____

_____

_____

_____

My 'WHY' Mission Statement
You 'Mission Statement' will define your 'why' and 'how'.

_____

_____

_____

_____

_____

_____

_____

_____

_____

"Change your thoughts and you can change the world."

~ Norman Vincent Peale

My skill set and expertise inventory

List all the skills and expertise you have that can be utilized in your business.

All your qualities (ask your friends):

_____
_____
_____
_____
_____

All your qualifications:

_____
_____
_____
_____
_____

All your work experience:

_____
_____
_____
_____

All the jobs you've had:

_____

_____

_____

_____

_____

_____

All the hobbies/passions you have:

_____

_____

_____

_____

_____

_____

Other things you know well or can do:

_____

_____

_____

_____

_____

_____

You must want it and you must be
willing to commit.

So... are you committed?

_____

(Yes or No)

MY CURRENT DEBTS

DATE _____

LIST ALL DEBTS TO BE PAID OFF   DATE TO PAY THEM OFF BY:

- ○ _____   _____
- ○ _____   _____
- ○ _____   _____
- ○ _____   _____
- ○ _____   _____
- ○ _____   _____
- ○ _____   _____

IDEALLY, YOU WILL BEGIN TO PUT ASIDE 10%-20% OF YOUR
PAYCHEQUE. USING "I" STATEMENTS, MAKE A PROMISE TO
YOURSELF BELOW TO MAKE IT HAPPEN

_____

_____

_____

_____

_____

_____

_____

_____

_____

AFFIRMATION

*The past no longer matters.
It has no control over me.
I am in total control of my
thoughts and actions.*

JOURNALING...

_____
_____
_____
_____
_____
_____
_____
_____
_____
_____
_____
_____
_____
_____
_____

A woman should be two things: who & what she wants."

~ Coco Chanel

PERSONAL DEVELOPMENT

SELF & MENTAL CARE

MONTHLY PRIORITIES

NOTES

MY INTENTION FOR THIS WEEK IS...

Your Intention sets the tone for the rest of the week.
Best day to make an intention is Monday morning.

_____

_____

_____

_____

WEEKLY GOAL SETTING

What are your 1 to 2 goals that you will set this week. make them
SMART. Specific - Measurable - Achievable - Realistic - Timely

GOAL #1

_____

_____

_____

_____

GOAL #2

_____

_____

_____

_____

WEEKLY GOAL REFLECTION

What did I achieve this week?

What did I learn this week?

What went well this week?

What was challenging this week?

Best moment of the week:

Intentions for next week:

MY INTENTION FOR THIS WEEK IS...

Your Intention sets the tone for the rest of the week.
Best day to make an intention is Monday morning.

_____

_____

_____

_____

WEEKLY GOAL SETTING

What are your 1 to 2 goals that you will set this week. make them
SMART. Specific - Measurable - Achievable - Realistic - Timely

GOAL #1

_____

_____

_____

_____

GOAL #2

_____

_____

_____

_____

WEEKLY GOAL REFLECTION

What did I achieve this week?

What did I learn this week?

What went well this week?

What was challenging this week?

Best moment of the week:

Intentions for next week:

Week 3

MY INTENTION FOR THIS WEEK IS...

Your Intention sets the tone for the rest of the week.
Best day to make an intention is Monday morning.

_____

_____

_____

_____

WEEKLY GOAL SETTING

What are your 1 to 2 goals that you will set this week. make them
SMART. Specific - Measurable - Achievable - Realistic - Timely

GOAL #1

_____

_____

_____

_____

GOAL #2

_____

_____

_____

_____

WEEKLY GOAL REFLECTION

What did I achieve this week?

What did I learn this week?

What went well this week?

What was challenging this week?

Best moment of the week:

Intentions for next week:

MY INTENTION FOR THIS WEEK IS...

Your Intention sets the tone for the rest of the week.
Best day to make an intention is Monday morning.

_____

_____

_____

_____

WEEKLY GOAL SETTING

What are your 1 to 2 goals that you will set this week. make them
SMART. Specific - Measurable - Achievable - Realistic - Timely

GOAL #1

_____

_____

_____

_____

GOAL #2

_____

_____

_____

_____

WEEKLY GOAL REFLECTION

What did I achieve this week?

What did I learn this week?

What went well this week?

What was challenging this week?

Best moment of the week:

Intentions for next week:

AFFIRMATION

I am a strong, beautiful, capable women, and I too, can do this!

JOURNALING...

2nd Month

"Am I good enough? YES, I am."

~ *Michelle Obama*

PERSONAL DEVELOPMENT

SELF & MENTAL CARE

MONTHLY PRIORITIES

NOTES

MY INTENTION FOR THIS WEEK IS...

Your Intention sets the tone for the rest of the week.
Best day to make an intention is Monday morning.

WEEKLY GOAL SETTING

What are your 1 to 2 goals that you will set this week. make them
SMART. Specific - Measurable - Achievable - Realistic - Timely

GOAL #1

GOAL #2

WEEKLY GOAL REFLECTION

What did I achieve this week?

What did I learn this week?

What went well this week?

What was challenging this week?

Best moment of the week:

Intentions for next week:

Week 6

MY INTENTION FOR THIS WEEK IS...

Your Intention sets the tone for the rest of the week.
Best day to make an intention is Monday morning.

_____

_____

_____

_____

WEEKLY GOAL SETTING

What are your 1 to 2 goals that you will set this week. make them
SMART. Specific - Measurable - Achievable - Realistic - Timely

GOAL #1

_____

_____

_____

_____

GOAL #2

_____

_____

_____

_____

WEEKLY GOAL REFLECTION

What did I achieve this week?

What did I learn this week?

What went well this week?

What was challenging this week?

Best moment of the week:

Intentions for next week:

MY INTENTION FOR THIS WEEK IS...

Your Intention sets the tone for the rest of the week.
Best day to make an intention is Monday morning.

WEEKLY GOAL SETTING

What are your 1 to 2 goals that you will set this week. make them
SMART. Specific - Measurable - Achievable - Realistic - Timely

GOAL #1

GOAL #2

WEEKLY GOAL REFLECTION

What did I achieve this week?

What did I learn this week?

What went well this week?

What was challenging this week?

Best moment of the week:

Intentions for next week:

MY INTENTION FOR THIS WEEK IS...

Your Intention sets the tone for the rest of the week.
Best day to make an intention is Monday morning.

_____

_____

_____

_____

WEEKLY GOAL SETTING

What are your 1 to 2 goals that you will set this week. make them
SMART. Specific - Measurable - Achievable - Realistic - Timely

GOAL #1

_____

_____

_____

_____

GOAL #2

_____

_____

_____

WEEKLY GOAL REFLECTION

What did I achieve this week?

What did I learn this week?

What went well this week?

What was challenging this week?

Best moment of the week:

Intentions for next week:

"Never doubt that you are powerful, valuable and deserving of every chance and opportunity in the world to pursue and achieve your dreams."

~ Unknown

JOURNALING...

_____
_____
_____
_____
_____
_____
_____
_____
_____
_____
_____

3rd Month

"Well-behaved women seldom make history."

~ Laurel Thatcher

PERSONAL DEVELOPMENT

SELF & MENTAL CARE

MONTHLY PRIORITIES

NOTES

Week 9

MY INTENTION FOR THIS WEEK IS...

Your Intention sets the tone for the rest of the week.
Best day to make an intention is Monday morning.

WEEKLY GOAL SETTING

What are your 1 to 2 goals that you will set this week. make them
SMART. Specific - Measurable - Achievable - Realistic - Timely

GOAL #1

GOAL #2

WEEKLY GOAL REFLECTION

What did I achieve this week?

What did I learn this week?

What went well this week?

What was challenging this week?

Best moment of the week:

Intentions for next week:

MY INTENTION FOR THIS WEEK IS...

Your Intention sets the tone for the rest of the week.
Best day to make an intention is Monday morning.

_____

_____

_____

_____

WEEKLY GOAL SETTING

What are your 1 to 2 goals that you will set this week. make them
SMART. Specific - Measurable - Achievable - Realistic - Timely

GOAL #1

_____

_____

_____

_____

GOAL #2

_____

_____

_____

_____

WEEKLY GOAL REFLECTION

What did I achieve this week?

What did I learn this week?

What went well this week?

What was challenging this week?

Best moment of the week:

Intentions for next week:

MY INTENTION FOR THIS WEEK IS...

Your Intention sets the tone for the rest of the week.
Best day to make an intention is Monday morning.

_____

_____

_____

_____

WEEKLY GOAL SETTING

What are your 1 to 2 goals that you will set this week. make them
SMART. Specific - Measurable - Achievable - Realistic - Timely

GOAL #1

_____

_____

_____

_____

GOAL #2

_____

_____

_____

_____

WEEKLY GOAL REFLECTION

What did I achieve this week?

What did I learn this week?

What went well this week?

What was challenging this week?

Best moment of the week:

Intentions for next week:

MY INTENTION FOR THIS WEEK IS...

Your Intention sets the tone for the rest of the week.
Best day to make an intention is Monday morning.

_____

_____

_____

_____

WEEKLY GOAL SETTING

What are your 1 to 2 goals that you will set this week. make them
SMART. Specific - Measurable - Achievable - Realistic - Timely

GOAL #1

_____

_____

_____

_____

GOAL #2

_____

_____

_____

_____

WEEKLY GOAL REFLECTION

What did I achieve this week?

What did I learn this week?

What went well this week?

What was challenging this week?

Best moment of the week:

Intentions for next week:

MY INTENTION FOR THIS WEEK IS...

Your Intention sets the tone for the rest of the week.
Best day to make an intention is Monday morning.

WEEKLY GOAL SETTING

What are your 1 to 2 goals that you will set this week. make them
SMART. Specific - Measurable - Achievable - Realistic - Timely

GOAL #1

GOAL #2

WEEKLY GOAL
REFLECTION

What did I achieve this week?

What did I learn this week?

What went well this week?

What was challenging this week?

Best moment of the week:

Intentions for next week:

DEBT CHECK-IN

DATE _____

LIST ALL DEBTS TO BE PAID OFF   DATE TO PAY THEM OFF BY:

○ _____   _____

○ _____   _____

○ _____   _____

○ _____   _____

○ _____   _____

○ _____   _____

○ _____   _____

IDEALLY, YOU WILL BEGIN TO PUT ASIDE 10%-20% OF YOUR
PAYCHEQUE. USING "I" STATEMENTS, MAKE A PROMISE TO
YOURSELF BELOW TO MAKE IT HAPPEN

_____

_____

_____

_____

_____

_____

_____

_____

_____

_____

_____

"Anything is possible if you have enough nerve."

~ J. K. Rowling

JOURNALING...

_____
_____
_____
_____
_____
_____
_____
_____
_____
_____
_____
_____
_____
_____
_____

4th Month

"You have to believe in yourself when no one else does."

~ Serena Williams

PERSONAL DEVELOPMENT

SELF & MENTAL CARE

MONTHLY PRIORITIES

NOTES

Week 14

MY INTENTION FOR THIS WEEK IS...

Your Intention sets the tone for the rest of the week.
Best day to make an intention is Monday morning.

WEEKLY GOAL SETTING

What are your 1 to 2 goals that you will set this week. make them
SMART. Specific - Measurable - Achievable - Realistic - Timely

GOAL #1

GOAL #2

WEEKLY GOAL REFLECTION

What did I achieve this week?

What did I learn this week?

What went well this week?

What was challenging this week?

Best moment of the week:

Intentions for next week:

MY INTENTION FOR THIS WEEK IS...

Your Intention sets the tone for the rest of the week.
Best day to make an intention is Monday morning.

_____

_____

_____

_____

WEEKLY GOAL SETTING

What are your 1 to 2 goals that you will set this week. make them
SMART. Specific - Measurable - Achievable - Realistic - Timely

GOAL #1

_____

_____

_____

_____

GOAL #2

_____

_____

_____

_____

WEEKLY GOAL REFLECTION

What did I achieve this week?

What did I learn this week?

What went well this week?

What was challenging this week?

Best moment of the week:

Intentions for next week:

MY INTENTION FOR THIS WEEK IS...

Your Intention sets the tone for the rest of the week.
Best day to make an intention is Monday morning.

_____

_____

_____

_____

WEEKLY GOAL SETTING

What are your 1 to 2 goals that you will set this week. make them
SMART. Specific - Measurable - Achievable - Realistic - Timely

GOAL #1

_____

_____

_____

_____

GOAL #2

_____

_____

_____

_____

WEEKLY GOAL REFLECTION

What did I achieve this week?

What did I learn this week?

What went well this week?

What was challenging this week?

Best moment of the week:

Intentions for next week:

Week 17

MY INTENTION FOR THIS WEEK IS...

Your Intention sets the tone for the rest of the week.
Best day to make an intention is Monday morning.

_____

_____

_____

_____

WEEKLY GOAL SETTING

What are your 1 to 2 goals that you will set this week. make them
SMART. Specific - Measurable - Achievable - Realistic - Timely

GOAL #1

_____

_____

_____

_____

GOAL #2

_____

_____

_____

_____

WEEKLY GOAL REFLECTION

What did I achieve this week?

What did I learn this week?

What went well this week?

What was challenging this week?

Best moment of the week:

Intentions for next week:

Time for Reflection

Now that you have spent some time journaling and recording your weekly goals, I am sure you have noticed that when you intentionally think about what you want to create, you begin to focus your thoughts on the things that bring you closer to your goal. Each week as you reflect on how much closer you are to building your business and creating freedom in your life, you become more confident in yourself and what you are able to accomplish.

Let me know where you are struggling. What would you like to know more about, what would help you take the first steps towards building your online business.

email me at karina@karinagsanchez.com

"Show me how good it can get!"

~ Unknown

JOURNALING...

5th Month

> "A woman with a voice is by definition a strong woman."
> ~ Melinda Gates

PERSONAL DEVELOPMENT

SELF & MENTAL CARE

MONTHLY PRIORITIES

NOTES

MY INTENTION FOR THIS WEEK IS...

Your Intention sets the tone for the rest of the week.
Best day to make an intention is Monday morning.

_____

_____

_____

_____

WEEKLY GOAL SETTING

What are your 1 to 2 goals that you will set this week. make them
SMART. Specific - Measurable - Achievable - Realistic - Timely

GOAL #1

_____

_____

_____

_____

GOAL #2

_____

_____

_____

_____

WEEKLY GOAL REFLECTION

What did I achieve this week?

What did I learn this week?

What went well this week?

What was challenging this week?

Best moment of the week:

Intentions for next week:

Week 19

MY INTENTION FOR THIS WEEK IS...

Your Intention sets the tone for the rest of the week.
Best day to make an intention is Monday morning.

_____

_____

_____

_____

WEEKLY GOAL SETTING

What are your 1 to 2 goals that you will set this week. make them
SMART. Specific - Measurable - Achievable - Realistic - Timely

GOAL #1

_____

_____

_____

GOAL #2

_____

_____

_____

WEEKLY GOAL REFLECTION

What did I achieve this week?

What did I learn this week?

What went well this week?

What was challenging this week?

Best moment of the week:

Intentions for next week:

MY INTENTION FOR THIS WEEK IS...

Your Intention sets the tone for the rest of the week.
Best day to make an intention is Monday morning.

WEEKLY GOAL SETTING

What are your 1 to 2 goals that you will set this week. make them
SMART. Specific - Measurable - Achievable - Realistic - Timely

GOAL #1

GOAL #2

WEEKLY GOAL REFLECTION

What did I achieve this week?

What did I learn this week?

What went well this week?

What was challenging this week?

Best moment of the week:

Intentions for next week:

MY INTENTION FOR THIS WEEK IS...

Your Intention sets the tone for the rest of the week.
Best day to make an intention is Monday morning.

WEEKLY GOAL SETTING

What are your 1 to 2 goals that you will set this week. make them
SMART. Specific - Measurable - Achievable - Realistic - Timely

GOAL #1

GOAL #2

WEEKLY GOAL
REFLECTION

What did I achieve this week?   What did I learn this week?

What went well this week?   What was challenging this week?

Best moment of the week: Intentions for next week:

"It always seems impossible until it's done."

~ Nelson Mandela

JOURNALING...

_____

_____

_____

_____

_____

_____

_____

_____

_____

_____

_____

_____

_____

_____

*"Don't follow the crowd,
let the crowd follow you."*

~ Margaret Thatcher

PERSONAL DEVELOPMENT

SELF & MENTAL CARE

MONTHLY PRIORITIES

NOTES

MY INTENTION FOR THIS WEEK IS...

Your Intention sets the tone for the rest of the week.
Best day to make an intention is Monday morning.

WEEKLY GOAL SETTING

What are your 1 to 2 goals that you will set this week. make them
SMART. Specific - Measurable - Achievable - Realistic - Timely

GOAL #1

GOAL #2

WEEKLY GOAL REFLECTION

What did I achieve this week?

What did I learn this week?

What went well this week?

What was challenging this week?

Best moment of the week:

Intentions for next week:

MY INTENTION FOR THIS WEEK IS...

Your Intention sets the tone for the rest of the week.
Best day to make an intention is Monday morning.

WEEKLY GOAL SETTING

What are your 1 to 2 goals that you will set this week. make them
SMART. Specific - Measurable - Achievable - Realistic - Timely

GOAL #1

GOAL #2

WEEKLY GOAL REFLECTION

What did I achieve this week?

What did I learn this week?

What went well this week?

What was challenging this week?

Best moment of the week:

Intentions for next week:

MY INTENTION FOR THIS WEEK IS...

Your Intention sets the tone for the rest of the week.
Best day to make an intention is Monday morning.

_____

_____

_____

_____

WEEKLY GOAL SETTING

What are your 1 to 2 goals that you will set this week. make them
SMART. Specific - Measurable - Achievable - Realistic - Timely

GOAL #1

_____

_____

_____

GOAL #2

_____

_____

_____

WEEKLY GOAL REFLECTION

What did I achieve this week?

What did I learn this week?

What went well this week?

What was challenging this week?

Best moment of the week:

Intentions for next week:

Week 25

MY INTENTION FOR THIS WEEK IS...

Your Intention sets the tone for the rest of the week.
Best day to make an intention is Monday morning.

_____

_____

_____

_____

WEEKLY GOAL SETTING

What are your 1 to 2 goals that you will set this week. make them
SMART. Specific - Measurable - Achievable - Realistic - Timely

GOAL #1

_____

_____

_____

_____

GOAL #2

_____

_____

_____

_____

WEEKLY GOAL REFLECTION

What did I achieve this week?

What did I learn this week?

What went well this week?

What was challenging this week?

Best moment of the week:

Intentions for next week:

Week 26

MY INTENTION FOR THIS WEEK IS...

Your Intention sets the tone for the rest of the week.
Best day to make an intention is Monday morning.

_____

_____

_____

_____

WEEKLY GOAL SETTING

What are your 1 to 2 goals that you will set this week. make them
SMART. Specific - Measurable - Achievable - Realistic - Timely

GOAL #1

_____

_____

_____

_____

GOAL #2

_____

_____

_____

_____

WEEKLY GOAL REFLECTION

What did I achieve this week?

What did I learn this week?

What went well this week?

What was challenging this week?

Best moment of the week:

Intentions for next week:

DEBT CHECK-IN

DATE _____

LIST ALL DEBTS TO BE PAID OFF	DATE TO PAY THEM OFF BY:
○	
○	
○	
○	
○	
○	
○	

IDEALLY, YOU WILL BEGIN TO PUT ASIDE 10%-20% OF YOUR PAYCHEQUE. USING "I" STATEMENTS, MAKE A PROMISE TO YOURSELF BELOW TO MAKE IT HAPPEN

_____

_____

_____

_____

_____

_____

_____

_____

_____

_____

"Define success on your own terms, achieve it by your own rules, life on your own terms."

~ Anne Sweeney

JOURNALING...

Life is either a daring adventure or nothing."

~ Helen Keller

PERSONAL DEVELOPMENT

SELF & MENTAL CARE

MONTHLY PRIORITIES

NOTES

Week 27

MY INTENTION FOR THIS WEEK IS...

Your Intention sets the tone for the rest of the week.
Best day to make an intention is Monday morning.

_____

_____

_____

_____

WEEKLY GOAL SETTING

What are your 1 to 2 goals that you will set this week. make them
SMART. Specific - Measurable - Achievable - Realistic - Timely

GOAL #1

_____

_____

_____

_____

GOAL #2

_____

_____

_____

_____

WEEKLY GOAL REFLECTION

What did I achieve this week?

What did I learn this week?

What went well this week?

What was challenging this week?

Best moment of the week:

Intentions for next week:

MY INTENTION FOR THIS WEEK IS...

Your Intention sets the tone for the rest of the week.
Best day to make an intention is Monday morning.

WEEKLY GOAL SETTING

What are your 1 to 2 goals that you will set this week. make them
SMART. Specific - Measurable - Achievable - Realistic - Timely

GOAL #1

GOAL #2

WEEKLY GOAL REFLECTION

What did I achieve this week?

What did I learn this week?

What went well this week?

What was challenging this week?

Best moment of the week:

Intentions for next week:

MY INTENTION FOR THIS WEEK IS...

Your Intention sets the tone for the rest of the week.
Best day to make an intention is Monday morning.

_____

_____

_____

_____

WEEKLY GOAL SETTING

What are your 1 to 2 goals that you will set this week. make them
SMART. Specific - Measurable - Achievable - Realistic - Timely

GOAL #1

_____

_____

_____

_____

GOAL #2

_____

_____

_____

_____

WEEKLY GOAL REFLECTION

What did I achieve this week?

What did I learn this week?

What went well this week?

What was challenging this week?

Best moment of the week:

Intentions for next week:

MY INTENTION FOR THIS WEEK IS...

Your Intention sets the tone for the rest of the week.
Best day to make an intention is Monday morning.

WEEKLY GOAL SETTING

What are your 1 to 2 goals that you will set this week. make them
SMART. Specific - Measurable - Achievable - Realistic - Timely

GOAL #1

GOAL #2

WEEKLY GOAL REFLECTION

What did I achieve this week?

What did I learn this week?

What went well this week?

What was challenging this week?

Best moment of the week:

Intentions for next week:

AFFIRMATION

I will not compare myself to anyone else because everyone is on their own journey.

JOURNALING...

Love yourself first and everything else falls into line."

~ Lucille Ball

PERSONAL DEVELOPMENT

SELF & MENTAL CARE

MONTHLY PRIORITIES

NOTES

MY INTENTION FOR THIS WEEK IS...

Your Intention sets the tone for the rest of the week.
Best day to make an intention is Monday morning.

_____

_____

_____

_____

WEEKLY GOAL SETTING

What are your 1 to 2 goals that you will set this week. make them
SMART. Specific - Measurable - Achievable - Realistic - Timely

GOAL #1

_____

_____

_____

_____

GOAL #2

_____

_____

_____

_____

WEEKLY GOAL REFLECTION

What did I achieve this week?

What did I learn this week?

What went well this week?

What was challenging this week?

Best moment of the week:

Intentions for next week:

MY INTENTION FOR THIS WEEK IS...

Your Intention sets the tone for the rest of the week.
Best day to make an intention is Monday morning.

WEEKLY GOAL SETTING

What are your 1 to 2 goals that you will set this week. make them
SMART. Specific - Measurable - Achievable - Realistic - Timely

GOAL #1

GOAL #2

WEEKLY GOAL REFLECTION

What did I achieve this week?

What did I learn this week?

What went well this week?

What was challenging this week?

Best moment of the week:

Intentions for next week:

MY INTENTION FOR THIS WEEK IS...

Your Intention sets the tone for the rest of the week.
Best day to make an intention is Monday morning.

WEEKLY GOAL SETTING

What are your 1 to 2 goals that you will set this week. make them
SMART. Specific - Measurable - Achievable - Realistic - Timely

GOAL #1

GOAL #2

WEEKLY GOAL REFLECTION

What did I achieve this week?

What did I learn this week?

What went well this week?

What was challenging this week?

Best moment of the week:

Intentions for next week:

Week 34

MY INTENTION FOR THIS WEEK IS...

Your Intention sets the tone for the rest of the week.
Best day to make an intention is Monday morning.

_____

_____

_____

_____

WEEKLY GOAL SETTING

What are your 1 to 2 goals that you will set this week. make them
SMART. Specific - Measurable - Achievable - Realistic - Timely

GOAL #1

_____

_____

_____

GOAL #2

_____

_____

_____

WEEKLY GOAL REFLECTION

What did I achieve this week?

What did I learn this week?

What went well this week?

What was challenging this week?

Best moment of the week:

Intentions for next week:

"Don't give up, don't take anything personally, and don't take NO for an answer."

~ Sophia Amoruso

JOURNALING...

9th Month

"I never dreamed about success. I worked for it."

~ Estee Lauder

PERSONAL DEVELOPMENT

SELF & MENTAL CARE

MONTHLY PRIORITIES

NOTES

MY INTENTION FOR THIS WEEK IS...

Your Intention sets the tone for the rest of the week.
Best day to make an intention is Monday morning.

_____

_____

_____

_____

WEEKLY GOAL SETTING

What are your 1 to 2 goals that you will set this week. make them
SMART. Specific - Measurable - Achievable - Realistic - Timely

GOAL #1

_____

_____

_____

_____

GOAL #2

_____

_____

_____

_____

WEEKLY GOAL REFLECTION

What did I achieve this week?

What did I learn this week?

What went well this week?

What was challenging this week?

Best moment of the week:

Intentions for next week:

Week 36

MY INTENTION FOR THIS WEEK IS...

Your Intention sets the tone for the rest of the week.
Best day to make an intention is Monday morning.

_____

_____

_____

_____

WEEKLY GOAL SETTING

What are your 1 to 2 goals that you will set this week. make them
SMART. Specific - Measurable - Achievable - Realistic - Timely

GOAL #1

_____

_____

_____

_____

GOAL #2

_____

_____

_____

_____

WEEKLY GOAL REFLECTION

What did I achieve this week?

What did I learn this week?

What went well this week?

What was challenging this week?

Best moment of the week:

Intentions for next week:

MY INTENTION FOR THIS WEEK IS...

Your Intention sets the tone for the rest of the week.
Best day to make an intention is Monday morning.

_____

_____

_____

_____

WEEKLY GOAL SETTING

What are your 1 to 2 goals that you will set this week. make them
SMART. Specific - Measurable - Achievable - Realistic - Timely

GOAL #1

_____

_____

_____

_____

GOAL #2

_____

_____

_____

_____

WEEKLY GOAL REFLECTION

What did I achieve this week?

What did I learn this week?

What went well this week?

What was challenging this week?

Best moment of the week:

Intentions for next week:

MY INTENTION FOR THIS WEEK IS...

Your Intention sets the tone for the rest of the week.
Best day to make an intention is Monday morning.

WEEKLY GOAL SETTING

What are your 1 to 2 goals that you will set this week. make them
SMART. Specific - Measurable - Achievable - Realistic - Timely

GOAL #1

GOAL #2

WEEKLY GOAL REFLECTION

What did I achieve this week?

What did I learn this week?

What went well this week?

What was challenging this week?

Best moment of the week:

Intentions for next week:

MY INTENTION FOR THIS WEEK IS...

Your Intention sets the tone for the rest of the week.
Best day to make an intention is Monday morning.

_____

_____

_____

_____

WEEKLY GOAL SETTING

What are your 1 to 2 goals that you will set this week. make them
SMART. Specific - Measurable - Achievable - Realistic - Timely

GOAL #1

_____

_____

_____

_____

GOAL #2

_____

_____

_____

_____

WEEKLY GOAL REFLECTION

What did I achieve this week?

What did I learn this week?

What went well this week?

What was challenging this week?

Best moment of the week:

Intentions for next week:

3rd Quarter
DEBT CHECK-IN

DATE _____

LIST ALL DEBTS TO BE PAID OFF   DATE TO PAY THEM OFF BY:

○ _____   _____

○ _____   _____

○ _____   _____

○ _____   _____

○ _____   _____

○ _____   _____

○ _____   _____

IDEALLY, YOU WILL BEGIN TO PUT ASIDE 10%-20% OF YOUR
PAYCHEQUE. USING "I" STATEMENTS, MAKE A PROMISE TO
YOURSELF BELOW TO MAKE IT HAPPEN

_____

_____

_____

_____

_____

_____

_____

_____

_____

_____

_____

"There is no limit to what 'we' women can accomplish."
~ Michelle Obama

PERSONAL DEVELOPMENT

SELF & MENTAL CARE

MONTHLY PRIORITIES

NOTES

Week 40

MY INTENTION FOR THIS WEEK IS...

Your Intention sets the tone for the rest of the week.
Best day to make an intention is Monday morning.

WEEKLY GOAL SETTING

What are your 1 to 2 goals that you will set this week. make them
SMART. Specific - Measurable - Achievable - Realistic - Timely

GOAL #1

GOAL #2

WEEKLY GOAL REFLECTION

What did I achieve this week?

What did I learn this week?

What went well this week?

What was challenging this week?

Best moment of the week:

Intentions for next week:

MY INTENTION FOR THIS WEEK IS...

Your Intention sets the tone for the rest of the week.
Best day to make an intention is Monday morning.

_____

_____

_____

_____

WEEKLY GOAL SETTING

What are your 1 to 2 goals that you will set this week. make them
SMART. Specific - Measurable - Achievable - Realistic - Timely

GOAL #1

_____

_____

_____

_____

GOAL #2

_____

_____

_____

_____

WEEKLY GOAL REFLECTION

What did I achieve this week?

What did I learn this week?

What went well this week?

What was challenging this week?

Best moment of the week:

Intentions for next week:

MY INTENTION FOR THIS WEEK IS...

Your Intention sets the tone for the rest of the week.
Best day to make an intention is Monday morning.

_____

_____

_____

_____

WEEKLY GOAL SETTING

What are your 1 to 2 goals that you will set this week. make them
SMART. Specific - Measurable - Achievable - Realistic - Timely

GOAL #1

_____

_____

_____

_____

GOAL #2

_____

_____

_____

_____

WEEKLY GOAL REFLECTION

What did I achieve this week?

What did I learn this week?

What went well this week?

What was challenging this week?

Best moment of the week:

Intentions for next week:

MY INTENTION FOR THIS WEEK IS...

Your Intention sets the tone for the rest of the week.
Best day to make an intention is Monday morning.

_____

_____

_____

_____

WEEKLY GOAL SETTING

What are your 1 to 2 goals that you will set this week. make them
SMART. Specific - Measurable - Achievable - Realistic - Timely

GOAL #1

_____

_____

_____

_____

GOAL #2

_____

_____

_____

_____

WEEKLY GOAL REFLECTION

What did I achieve this week?

What did I learn this week?

What went well this week?

What was challenging this week?

Best moment of the week:

Intentions for next week:

"You are more powerful than you know."

~ Melissa Etheridge

JOURNALING...

_____

_____

_____

_____

_____

_____

_____

_____

_____

_____

_____

_____

_____

_____

_____

11th Month

PERSONAL DEVELOPMENT

SELF & MENTAL CARE

MONTHLY PRIORITIES

NOTES

Week 44

MY INTENTION FOR THIS WEEK IS...

Your Intention sets the tone for the rest of the week.
Best day to make an intention is Monday morning.

_____

_____

_____

_____

WEEKLY GOAL SETTING

What are your 1 to 2 goals that you will set this week. make them
SMART. Specific - Measurable - Achievable - Realistic - Timely

GOAL #1

_____

_____

_____

_____

GOAL #2

_____

_____

_____

_____

WEEKLY GOAL REFLECTION

What did I achieve this week?

What did I learn this week?

What went well this week?

What was challenging this week?

Best moment of the week:

Intentions for next week:

MY INTENTION FOR THIS WEEK IS...

Your Intention sets the tone for the rest of the week.
Best day to make an intention is Monday morning.

_____

_____

_____

_____

WEEKLY GOAL SETTING

What are your 1 to 2 goals that you will set this week. make them
SMART. Specific - Measurable - Achievable - Realistic - Timely

GOAL #1

_____

_____

_____

_____

GOAL #2

_____

_____

_____

_____

WEEKLY GOAL REFLECTION

What did I achieve this week?

What did I learn this week?

What went well this week?

What was challenging this week?

Best moment of the week:

Intentions for next week:

Week 46

MY INTENTION FOR THIS WEEK IS...

Your Intention sets the tone for the rest of the week.
Best day to make an intention is Monday morning.

_____

_____

_____

_____

WEEKLY GOAL SETTING

What are your 1 to 2 goals that you will set this week. make them
SMART. Specific - Measurable - Achievable - Realistic - Timely

GOAL #1

_____

_____

_____

_____

GOAL #2

_____

_____

_____

_____

WEEKLY GOAL REFLECTION

What did I achieve this week?

What did I learn this week?

What went well this week?

What was challenging this week?

Best moment of the week:

Intentions for next week:

MY INTENTION FOR THIS WEEK IS...

Your Intention sets the tone for the rest of the week.
Best day to make an intention is Monday morning.

_____

_____

_____

_____

WEEKLY GOAL SETTING

What are your 1 to 2 goals that you will set this week. make them
SMART. Specific - Measurable - Achievable - Realistic - Timely

GOAL #1

_____

_____

_____

_____

GOAL #2

_____

_____

_____

_____

WEEKLY GOAL REFLECTION

What did I achieve this week?

What did I learn this week?

What went well this week?

What was challenging this week?

Best moment of the week:

Intentions for next week:

AFFIRMATION

I believe in myself and I believe in the path I have chosen. My path will lead to my goals.

JOURNALING...

The biggest barrier for women is to think that they can't have it all."

~ Coco Chanel

PERSONAL DEVELOPMENT

SELF & MENTAL CARE

MONTHLY PRIORITIES

NOTES

MY INTENTION FOR THIS WEEK IS...

Your Intention sets the tone for the rest of the week.
Best day to make an intention is Monday morning.

WEEKLY GOAL SETTING

What are your 1 to 2 goals that you will set this week. make them
SMART. Specific - Measurable - Achievable - Realistic - Timely

GOAL #1

GOAL #2

WEEKLY GOAL REFLECTION

What did I achieve this week?

What did I learn this week?

What went well this week?

What was challenging this week?

Best moment of the week:

Intentions for next week:

MY INTENTION FOR THIS WEEK IS...

Your Intention sets the tone for the rest of the week.
Best day to make an intention is Monday morning.

WEEKLY GOAL SETTING

What are your 1 to 2 goals that you will set this week. make them
SMART. Specific - Measurable - Achievable - Realistic - Timely

GOAL #1

GOAL #2

WEEKLY GOAL REFLECTION

What did I achieve this week?

What did I learn this week?

What went well this week?

What was challenging this week?

Best moment of the week:

Intentions for next week:

MY INTENTION FOR THIS WEEK IS...

Your Intention sets the tone for the rest of the week.
Best day to make an intention is Monday morning.

WEEKLY GOAL SETTING

What are your 1 to 2 goals that you will set this week. make them
SMART. Specific - Measurable - Achievable - Realistic - Timely

GOAL #1

GOAL #2

WEEKLY GOAL REFLECTION

What did I achieve this week?

What did I learn this week?

What went well this week?

What was challenging this week?

Best moment of the week:

Intentions for next week:

Week 51

MY INTENTION FOR THIS WEEK IS...

Your Intention sets the tone for the rest of the week.
Best day to make an intention is Monday morning.

_____

_____

_____

_____

WEEKLY GOAL SETTING

What are your 1 to 2 goals that you will set this week. make them
SMART. Specific - Measurable - Achievable - Realistic - Timely

GOAL #1

_____

_____

_____

_____

GOAL #2

_____

_____

_____

_____

WEEKLY GOAL REFLECTION

What did I achieve this week?

What did I learn this week?

What went well this week?

What was challenging this week?

Best moment of the week:

Intentions for next week:

MY INTENTION FOR THIS WEEK IS...

Your Intention sets the tone for the rest of the week.
Best day to make an intention is Monday morning.

_____

_____

_____

_____

WEEKLY GOAL SETTING

What are your 1 to 2 goals that you will set this week. make them
SMART. Specific - Measurable - Achievable - Realistic - Timely

GOAL #1

_____

_____

_____

_____

GOAL #2

_____

_____

_____

_____

WEEKLY GOAL REFLECTION

What did I achieve this week?

What did I learn this week?

What went well this week?

What was challenging this week?

Best moment of the week:

Intentions for next week:

4th Quarter
DEBT CHECK-IN

DATE _____

LIST ALL DEBTS TO BE PAID OFF

○ _____

○ _____

○ _____

○ _____

○ _____

○ _____

○ _____

DATE TO PAY THEM OFF BY:

_____

_____

_____

_____

_____

_____

_____

IDEALLY, YOU WILL BEGIN TO PUT ASIDE 10%-20% OF YOUR PAYCHEQUE. USING "I" STATEMENTS, MAKE A PROMISE TO YOURSELF BELOW TO MAKE IT HAPPEN

_____

_____

_____

_____

_____

_____

_____

_____

_____

_____

AFFIRMATION

I will award and praise myself for my accomplishments. I deserve good things in my life and I work towards my success.

JOURNALING...

Conclusion

This is it! You know what you need to do. There is no more wondering in the dark. You can trust yourself because now this information is ingrained in your mind, deep in your mind. You can do these check-ins every time you need them and you can set your weekly goals all by yourself now. I believe in you and you need to believe in yourself.

The world is your oyster. You find your pearl. Be bold, persist and you will achieve your goals. I know this like I know that life is what you make it, so make it the best one you will ever have!

"You'll never do a whole lot unless you are brave enough to try."

~ Dolly Parton

www.ingramcontent.com/pod-product-compliance
Lightning Source LLC
Chambersburg PA
CBHW061023220326
41597CB00019BB/3072